REBUILDING THE RENAISSANCE

※ VOLUME I ※

The Ancient Roman World

Rocky Ruggiero™

MAKING ART AND HISTORY COME TO LIFE

**Rebuilding the Renaissance:
Volume I, The Ancient Roman World**
Copyright © 2025 Rocky Ruggiero

Produced and printed by Stillwater River Publications.
All rights reserved. Written and produced in the United States
of America. This book may not be reproduced or sold in any
form without the expressed, written permission
of the author and publisher.

Visit our website at
www.StillwaterPress.com
for more information.

First Stillwater River Publications Edition.

ISBN: 978-1-965733-64-6

Library of Congress Control Number: 2025907996

1 2 3 4 5 6 7 8 9 10

Written by Dr. Rocky Ruggiero.
Cover and interior book design by Matthew St. Jean.
Published by Stillwater River Publications,
West Warwick, RI, USA.

Publisher's Cataloging-in-Publication
(Provided by Cassidy Cataloguing Services, Inc.)
Names: Ruggiero, Rocky, author.
Title: Rebuilding the Renaissance. Volume I,
The ancient world / Rocky Ruggiero.
Other titles: Ancient world
Description: First Stillwater River Publications edition. |
West Warwick, RI, USA : Stillwater River Publications, [2025]
Identifiers: LCCN: 2025907996 | ISBN: 9781965733646 (paperback)
Subjects: LCSH: Renaissance--Italy. | Art--Italy--History. |
Architecture--Italy--History. | Art--Rome--History. |
Architecture--Rome--History. | Italy--Civilization. |
Italy--History. | Rome--Civilization. | Rome--History.
Classification: LCC: DG445 .R84 2025 |
DDC: 945.05--dc23

*The views and opinions expressed in this book are solely
those of the author and do not necessarily reflect the
views and opinions of the publisher.*

REBUILDING THE RENAISSANCE

CONTENTS

Foreword by Ross King   vii
Preface by Dr. Rocky Ruggiero   ix

1. The Foundation Myth   1
2. Julius Caesar and the Dawn of an Empire   15
3. The Colosseum   31
4. Blood Sport   43
5. Bread & Circus   55
6. The Pantheon   61
7. Constantine & Christianity   77
8. Ravenna: The Byzantine Empire Strikes Back   91
9. The Ancient Roman Origins of Florence   101

About the Author...   *117*

FOREWORD

Few cities in the world are as captivating as Rome—with its bizarre foundation myths, its cast of heroes and villains, its astonishing cruelty, awe-inspiring territorial conquests, breathtaking architecture, and a legacy that continues to shape our world today. Dr. Rocky Ruggiero masterfully brings it all together in a lively narrative filled with illuminating insights and a series of stunning illustrations.

Fans of Dr. Rocky Ruggiero's lectures, podcasts, or tours are familiar with his depth of knowledge, knack for uncovering fascinating little-known details, up-to-date scholarship, and, of course, his lashings of humor. Now, these qualities are available in book form, offering a vivid and engaging exploration of the grandeur (and sometimes the horror) that was Ancient Rome.

Dr. Ruggiero places iconic monuments like the Colosseum and the Pantheon into their rich historical context, expertly recounting their backstories and populating them with the Romans themselves—emperors, gladiators, and everyday citizens. Beyond the glory, he also examines Rome's weakness and vulnerability, tracing the Empire's conversion to Christianity, its slide into decay, and its eventual collapse under the weight of barbarian invasions—showing how even the mightiest civilizations can falter.

As always, Dr. Ruggiero breathes life into art and history, making them not only memorable but irresistibly enjoyable. Whether you're a seasoned history buff or simply curious about Rome's astonishing past, this book is the perfect companion to a cappuccino in the Campo de'Fiori—or wherever your imagination takes you.

Ross King
Author, *Brunelleschi's Dome* and
The Shortest History of Italy

PREFACE

Since 1994, I have been studying and teaching the Italian Renaissance—however, Ancient Rome has always been my secret passion. The legends, monuments, and astonishing history all make for what I believe to be is the most fascinating of historical epochs. Names and places familiar to us all, but whose true significance escapes most. Because it's only when we start to realize just how much of the modern western world was shaped by Ancient Rome, that we begin to understand that once we were all Romans!

Romans, who 2,800 years ago decided to transform a cluster of hills surrounding a swamp into one of the world's largest cities with a population of more than a million. Romans who experimented with monarchy until it developed into tyranny and then transformed it into democracy under the immortal acronym—SPQR. Romans who thought it was their manifest destiny to spread democracy, justice, order, and peace throughout the ancient world. Who slowly but surely but surely defeated all comers—Etruscans, Carthaginians, Greeks, Gauls, Druids, Parthians, and Germanic tribes alike. Who spread their control over nearly half of the known world, with borders as far reaching as Scotland, Egypt, the Atlantic Ocean, and the Persian Gulf. Romans who, to control this vast territory, constructed enough roads to wrap around the earth ten times. Who, to show their greatness, built gobsmacking monuments to their gods, themselves, and their achievements.

Romans who have left an indelible mark on our western collective consciousnesses. Whether it's chariot races, slave revolts, Egyptian queens, the birth and death of Christ, betrayed generals, deranged emperors, gladiators, or volcanic eruptions, we all inevitably flock to the cinema, theater, or bookstore for a glimpse of that world which we intuitively know as the ancestor of our own.

This is the story that I am going to tell you—the rise, domination, and fall of one of the greatest civilizations in history…and what eventually rose from the ashes.

How lucky am I? It's a story so great that it gives me goosebumps even when I'm only telling you how great it is. How humbled am I? To attempt to cover more than a millennium of art, architecture, and history in just a few pages.

How excited am I? Well, I think you will see that come through in the pages of this book. A book which is the first of several volumes dedicated to reconstructing that era which marked the rebirth of Greco-Roman antiquity and the birth of our own modern world.

In other words, dedicated to *Rebuilding the Renaissance.*

Rocky Ruggiero, PhD
December 2024

REBUILDING THE RENAISSANCE

Opposite: Forum Romanus, 7th century BCE. *Background:* Curia Julia, where the Senate made laws; the supreme court. *Foreground:* Temple of Saturn. *Center:* Arch of Septimus Severus. *Left:* Temple of Castor and Pollux.

CHAPTER 1

THE FOUNDATION MYTH

In every myth and in every legend, no matter how fantastical, there exists a certain degree of truth. So holds true for the great foundation myth of Rome. Historically, the Romans are not alone in creating this genus, a storyline that explains their significance and contribution to world history.

Another example is the foundation myth of Renaissance Florence, which serves as an historical apologia, a formal defense for its greatness. When the city's economy began to resurge in the Middle Ages, Florentines naturally looked to their past to investigate who they were and where they came from. What motivated this search for a historical identity was the wide-spread socioeconomic well-being of the city. Florentines came to realize that they were once Romans since their city had been founded as an ancient Roman colony. Therefore, Florence's magnificence could be simply explained as a consequence of being a daughter of Rome.

This deep-diving into a culture's past has continued over the centuries and is evidenced by the current craze over companies such as Ancestry.com and 23andMe.

After numerous generations of immigrants arriving on American shores, working tirelessly so their offspring might have

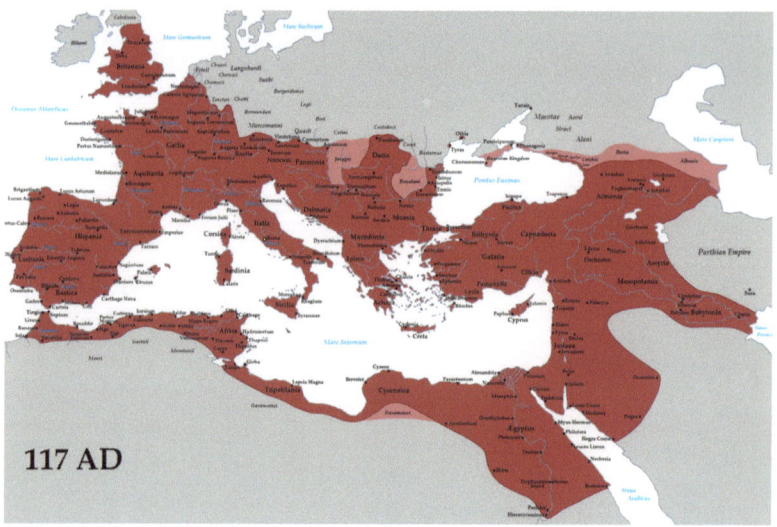

117 AD

a better life, many Americans now have the luxury of looking back to rediscover their roots. Most people like knowing where they come from—to have a sense of legacy or ancestry—which, in turn, serves as the foundation of their identities.

That is essentially what the ancient Romans sought to do in fashioning their own epic foundation myth. The Roman foundation myth was officially codified in the 1st century CE. By this time, Rome had become a vast empire, stretching over nearly half of the known world. The northernmost border of the Roman Empire was Hadrian's Wall, which is still largely preserved and lies between the borders of England and Scotland.

The western border of the Roman Empire reached to the edge of the Iberian Peninsula where it meets the Atlantic Ocean.

Most of northern Africa was also under Roman control, reaching southern Egypt and as far west as Morocco. The eastern border of the Roman Empire was located between the Tigris and Euphrates Rivers, between the modern nations of Iraq and Iran.

Imagine the implications of controlling such a vast territory two millennia ago without the aid of modern technology. No phones, no cable, no Internet.

So how did Rome come to control half of the world? Roads.

The cliché that "all roads lead to Rome" is, in fact, factual. The Romans laid more than 400,000 kilometers of roadways, nearly 90,000 of which were paved in stone. This network wove throughout their territory, giving them a tremendous advantage in communications and moving their legions more quickly and effectively than their adversaries.

Once Roman society realized that it was the dominant military force, controlling nearly half of the known world, it became essential for the Romans to look back to establish an official story of who they were, where they came from and how their story—their official foundation myth—explained a predestined power for their great city and eventual empire.

Not surprisingly, the foundation myth of Rome begins long before Roman history was written down—back to the legendary city of Troy. It was in the 1st century CE that the Roman author Virgil penned "The Aeneid," which recounts the heroic story of Aeneas who fled the burning city of Troy after it had fallen to the Greeks via the cunning scheme of the infamous Trojan Horse.

"The Aeneid" is anything but a dry high school assignment. It has all the elements and drama of a Hollywood screenplay—sex, murder and betrayal. Aeneas, along with his father Anchises, and his son, Ascanius, who were members of the junior branch of the royal Trojan family, fled the city to search for an ideal place where they could establish new Troy.

According to Virgil, Aeneas explored various locations, the island of Crete, then Carthage, then Sicily. All locations that would inevitably become superpowers of the ancient world, some of which would challenge the authority and the dominance of Rome, particularly Carthage. However, there could only be one Rome. That is why Aeneas eventually settled in an area on the Italic peninsula. His choice, the Alban Hills, is situated 12 miles southeast of Rome. This is where Aeneas fought for supremacy and eventually established his son, Ascanius, as the first king. Ascanius was also known as "Iulus," which is the source of the "nomen" or Roman name indicating a family descending from a common ancestor.

Ascanius' rule was followed by a series of successors...

Numitor became king of the Alban Hills but was later deposed by his ambitious younger brother Amulius, who was fearful that Numitor's newly born twin grandsons, Romulus and Remus, would one day seek revenge on behalf of their deposed grandfather. The mother of Romulus and Remus was Rhea Silvia (allegedly a Vestal Virgin).

According to myth, Rhea Silvia was "loved" by Mars, the Roman god of war, the offspring of which consummation was the predestined twins. Mars' lineage was not the only divine blood flowing through the veins of Numitor's grandsons. Think back to Aeneas, who was the son of the goddess Venus and a direct ancestor of the twin boys.

Therefore, Romulus and Remus were descended from two divine beings—Mars, the god of war, and Venus, the goddess

Gian Lorenzo Bernini, *Aeneas, Anchises, and Ascanius,* 1618, marble, 220 cm, Borghese Gallery, Rome.

Romulus and Remus
THE FAMILY TREE

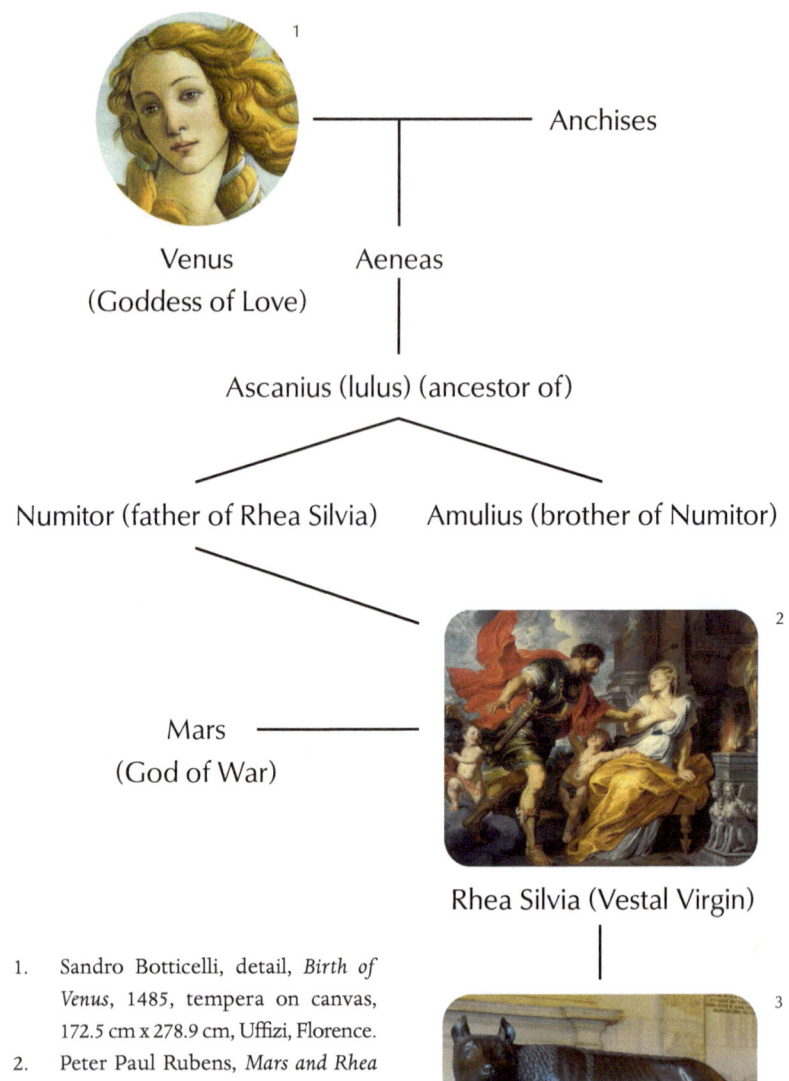

1. Sandro Botticelli, detail, *Birth of Venus*, 1485, tempera on canvas, 172.5 cm x 278.9 cm, Uffizi, Florence.
2. Peter Paul Rubens, *Mars and Rhea Silvia*, ca.1617/1620, oil on canvas, 208 cm x 272 cm, Liechtenstein Museum, Vienna.
3. Unown (wolf) and Antonio del Pollaiuolo (twins), *Capitoline Wolf*, 5th century BCE, bronze, 75 cm x 114 cm, Capitoline Museums, Rome.

View from the Capitoline Hill.

of love. Rome did imagine itself as a perfect societal dichotomy between love and war—either at peace or at war. However, Venus and Mars—love and war—were further unified by the match between Mars and Rhea Silvia, manifested by their twin sons, Romulus and Remus. The foundation plot thickens even more.

After the birth of the twins, their ruthless uncle, Amulius, decided they were a serious threat to his rule.

Fearful of divine wrath if he should harm them directly, he put the twin boys in a basket and set them afloat on the Tiber River, confident that the newborns would meet their end (Moses archetype?).

But the basket became entangled in the roots of a fig tree at the base of the Palatine Hill where the boys were discovered by a she-wolf. She nursed them as her own until a shepherd named Faustulus took in the two boys and raised them.

When the boys came of age, and after reinstating their

Nicolas Mignard, *The Shepherd Faustulus Bringing Romulus and Remus to His Fife*, 1654, oil on canvas, 148.5 x 145.1 cm, Dallas Museum of Art, Dallas.

grandfather, Numitor, as the king of the Alban Hills, they set off to establish their own city.

However, as brothers will do, they disagreed about where the new city should be located-Romulus contending the Palatine Hill while Remus chose the Aventine Hill. When they arrived at this decision, the quarreling brothers parted ways. Because they could not come to an agreement, they decided to consult the divine omens in the form of auguries-or the flights of birds, which was a means of communication in the ancient world.

The two then set about constructing their dwellings and waiting for a divine omen to appear. An omen did indeed come.

Remus looked into the sky and saw a flock of six vultures flying overhead, which he interpreted as a positive sign from the gods. He ran up to the Palatine Hill to inform his brother, unaware that in the meantime, Romulus had spotted a divine omen of his own—a flock of twelve vultures flying overhead! Naturally, an argument ensued over which was more important.

Who had seen the vultures first or who had seen more vultures? First or foremost? Quantity versus quality?

As the dispute intensified, it eventually degenerated into a physical altercation between the two and in the heat of the struggle, Romulus killed his brother Remus, and by default became the first king of Rome. (Cain and Abel archetype?)

A later Roman historian would justify this celebrated act of fratricide and assert that Remus had deserved his fate. He argued that because Remus had jumped over the walls his brother was building, he had behaved not as a brother but as an enemy. According to this historian, only enemies jump over walls as Remus had done while allies enter through doorways.

Thus, in the eyes of the Romans, Remus' act of trespassing served as justification for Romulus' act of fratricide. Romans recognize April 21, 753 BCE, as the date of this occurrence and proclaimed it the official birth date of their great city.

Following Remus' death, Romulus declared the area between the Palatine Hill and the Capitoline Hill in Rome an asylum, freely offering citizenship to all. Many young men joined Romulus' primitive society, but a significant problem quickly arose-there was a severe shortage of women.

Romulus realized that if he wanted his new city to prosper, he would need to recruit the fairer sex. He did so by asking the neighboring tribes where he could find the most beautiful, virtuous and fertile women in the area.

The answer was always the same-the Sabine hills. Romulus concocted a plan to host a lush feast on the Palatine Hill, inviting

Giambologna, *Abduction of a Sabine Woman*, 1579-1583, marble, 410 cm, Loggia dei Lanzi, Florence.

the Sabines to join. The Sabines did indeed show up to Romulus' party and at the height of the festivities, when all the Sabine men had drunk to excess, the Roman men drew their swords, killed the Sabine men and made off with the Sabine women. This infamous episode is usually referred to as "the rape of the Sabine," with the word "rape"—from the Latin "raptus"—in this context, meaning kidnapping or seizure. As a result, Rome now had the best men and the best women to produce an extraordinary society.

Romulus was the first king of Rome, and his rule was succeeded by a series of six more. Each of these six kings would make a major contribution to the historical identity of Rome. The immediate successor of Romulus was Numa Pompilius, who introduced the concept called "religio"—the root of "religion" which translates as "fear" or "awe" of the gods. Another king introduced military organization fundamental to Rome's military supremacy.

Yet another king drained the area today known as the Forum, the downtown area of Rome.

The seventh king, "Tarquin the Proud" or Tarquin Superbus in Latin, brought another surprising aspect to Roman society—the bitter taste of "tyranny." Tarquin the Proud was an Etruscan and ruled Rome as a tyrant. He imposed severe laws and abused his power.

His son Sextus Tarquinius raped Lucretia, the most virtuous woman in Rome. This violent act caused her to publicly denounce her disgrace and take her own life. Following this transgression, the people of Rome drove the Tarquin clan out of the city and transformed the monarchy into a republic in 509 BCE.

This is when the famous acronym, SPQR, Senatus Populusque Romanus ("The Senate and the People of Rome") was established and marked the beginning of another phase of Roman history. This Republican phase of history would last for approximately five centuries and would end with the rise of Gaius Julius Caesar.

SPQR plaque engraved on stone.

At what point does myth evolve into factual history? When were divine beings replaced by mortals? The archetypes (virgin birth, infants sent down the river and a brother killing another) are part of the fabric of humanity. Our common heritage, whether fact or fiction, is what creates the mental concepts and transforming power of art and history, interwoven into our communal story; the very kernel of the collective unconscious.

It is what makes art and history come to life!

Opposite: Mariano Rossi, *The Apotheosis of Romulus*, 1775-1779, fresco, Borghese Gallery, Rome.

Opposite: Unknown artist, *Lanuvium Claudius*, ca. 42-43 CE, marble, 254 cm, Vatican Museums, Rome. Photo by lbphoto.

CHAPTER 2

JULIUS CAESAR AND THE DAWN OF AN EMPIRE

The Roman Republic lasted for nearly five centuries, from 509 to 27 BCE. When the Roman Senate gave overarching political and martial power to the maternal nephew of Julius Caesar, Gaius Octavian, it effectively transformed the republic into an imperial monarchy.

After several name changes, Octavian eventually became known as "Imperator Caesar Augustus." The story of how that transition took place is one of the most dramatic and well-known accounts in history. Yet, while most people realize Julius Caesar (100-44 BCE) was largely responsible for the transformation of the Roman Republic into a monarchy, they are often surprised to discover he was not, in fact, the first "Emperor" of Rome. The ruling body of the Roman Republic was its Senate, whose members came from the city's patrician class. The two "executive" figures in the Senate were known as the "consuls."

They were always two in number so their power could be reciprocally checked. In addition to the Senate, there were other various legislative assemblies and magistrates who were also responsible for governing what was an ever rapidly growing territory controlled by Rome.

Yet, as Rome went through some of its most turbulent historical military challenges-first with the Etruscans, then later with the Carthaginians in the Punic Wars-it became increasingly effective to put absolute power temporarily into the hands of one man known as the "Dictator."

The Dictator was a magistrate of the Roman Republic entrusted with the full authority of the state to deal with a military emergency or to undertake a specific duty. The intent of this extraordinary role was to temporarily suspend the day-to-day bureaucracy typical of the republic when not in a state of emergency. While Rome was indeed a republic, it had, in its most trying times, turned to the rule of one, better known as monarchy.

Julius Caesar's rise to power began in a very unpromising way. His uncle Marius was on the losing side of a civil war known as the "Social War" (91–87 BCE). As a result, Caesar himself was proscribed, meaning that he had been publicly designated to be executed or banished. However, his mother's political connections intervened to have the condemnation lifted. After many years serving in the military and then as a successful lawyer, in

44 BCE denarius.

64 BCE, Caesar was elected to the position of *aedile,* the political figure responsible for public spectacles. This position gained him important political support on a popular level due to the spectacular nature of the events he organized.

In 60 BCE, Caesar was elected consul for the following year. He was also able to form an informal alliance between himself and two other powerful men, Pompey the Great and Markus Licinius Crassus. This tripartite alliance was known as "The First Triumvirate." Pompey the Great was one of Rome's greatest military leaders. He boasted to having conquered the three continents of Europe, Africa and Asia. Markus Licinius Crassus, on the other hand, was Rome's wealthiest citizen. The pact between these three figures ensured greater, albeit exclusive, political stability. Of the three members of the triumvirate, Caesar was by far the most ambitious and the most fortunate.

The next year, 59 BCE, Caesar marched four Roman legions, roughly 18,000 men, north over the Alps into a part of the world

Left: *The Chiaramonti Caesar,* ca. 30-20 BCE., marble, Vatican Museum, Rome.
Center: Bust of Pompey, copy of an original from 70-60 BCE., marble, Venice National Archaeological Museum, Venice.
Right: Bust found on the Lincian Tombs, traditionally identified as Marcus Licinius Crassus, marble, Glyptothek, Copenhagen.

referred to as "Transalpine Gaul" (an area of western Europe consisting of France, parts of Belgium and western Germany).

Caesar began what was up until then the most successful military campaign in the history of Rome, conquering all modern-day France and Belgium, touching upon Germany, Switzerland and Austria, and in 55 BCE eventually making his way across the English Channel to the mysterious island of Britannia.

Although he made little territorial conquest on the island, the sensational nature of the campaign quickly made Caesar a legend.

One victory after another and tales of near-defeat transformed to awe-inspiring victories enthused the Roman mob but terrified the Roman Senate. Fearful that one man was becoming too powerful too quickly, Caesar's domestic enemies became far more dangerous to him than the barbarian tribes he faced daily in battle.

While Caesar was assembling a successful military campaign, the triumvirate was rapidly coming undone. When Caesar was in Britain, his daughter Julia, wife of his ally, Pompey the Great, had died in childbirth. Caesar quickly offered his great niece in marriage to Pompey to maintain their alliance. Pompey declined his offer. His refusal was a clear message regarding his growing dissatisfaction over Caesar's unhinged power. After the ignominious defeat and death of Crassus at the Battle of Carrhae in 53 BCE, the First Triumvirate effectively came to an end. With the dissolution of the informal alliance, Rome was on the brink of civil war.

In 50 BCE, Caesar's governorship over Gaul ended, so the Senate ordered him to disband his army and to return to Rome. Such a move would have most likely meant a certain end to Caesar's political career and perhaps his very life. His enemies in the Senate would have most certainly tried him on criminal charges. Pompey went so far as to accuse Caesar of treason and would have punished him at the very least with exile and, at worst, execution.

Caesar and his closest ally, the Roman general Mark Antony,

Portrait bust of Marcus Antonius, ca. 69-96 CE, marble, Vatican Museums, Rome.

had taken up winter quarters in northeastern Italy, just north of a river that marked the boundary of what was then Cisalpine Gaul. That river, later immortalized by William Shakespeare in his renowned play *Julius Caesar*, was indeed the Rubicon River. In January 49 BCE, Caesar found himself at a critical turning point.

Should he go back to Rome without the protection of his legions, it would have led to personal and political disaster. Should he instead march his troops to Rome, he would have triggered a new Roman civil war.

On January 10 of the same year, Caesar uttered the famous words *alea iacta esto*-"the die is cast." With a single legion (the Legio XIII Gemina), he crossed the Rubicon River, defying the Senate and igniting civil war.

This maneuver took Rome completely by surprise. The Senate immediately asked Pompey to organize Rome's defense, but had little faith in his freshly trained troops. Aware of their vulnerability, most of the Senate and Pompey himself fled Rome.

When Caesar arrived unchallenged, he was appointed Dictator. He then appointed Mark Antony as "Master of

Unknown artist, bust of Julius Caesar.

Jean-Léon Gérôme, *Cleopatra and Caesar*, 1866,
oil on canvas, 183 cm x 129.5 cm, private collection.

the Horse" or "Second in Command," and left Rome in hot pursuit of Pompey and the fugitive Senators.

It was in Greece that Caesar and Antony would confront and eventually defeat Pompey, the Senate and their army, ultimately turning the tide of the civil war.

Having no where else to turn, Pompey thought he would find safety in Rome's old north African ally, Egypt, which was engaged in its own civil war. The ruling Pharaoh, Ptolemy XIII, and his half-sister, the celebrated Cleopatra, both of whom were Greek, were both vying for the throne.

The Ptolemaic Dynasty had been established by Alexander the Great centuries before. Pompey was initially welcomed by Ptolemy XIII, but in a bid to curry favor with Rome's soon-to-be-emperor, Caesar, Ptolemy had Pompey assassinated.

When Caesar finally arrived in Egypt he was presented with Pompey's severed head and seal ring, which he allegedly accepted in tears. Afterward, he would have Pompey's assassins executed, appalled that Egyptians would lay hands upon a Roman, particularly one of Pompey's distinguished rank.

Instead of returning to Rome after the death of his rival, Caesar instead took on the affairs of a foreign county. He became embroiled in the Egyptian civil war, initially trying to negotiate peace between the warring Ptolemaic siblings, but eventually siding with Cleopatra with whom he had become enamored.

Cleopatra's brilliance and persona enchanted him, preventing his return to Rome. After establishing her as sovereign of Egypt, Caesar, his client queen Cleopatra, and Caesarion, their newly born son, finally set sail for Rome.

Caesar imagined the Romans would be enthusiastic over the boy who carried the blood of two great ancient empires, Egypt and Rome. However, when the threesome arrived, they received a most unfriendly welcome.

The Romans were horrified, fearful that an Egyptian could

now legitimately lay claim to rule of Rome. While Caesar was heralded, Cleopatra and her son were effectively marginalized.

After resolving the civil conflict in Egypt, Caesar sought to do the same in Rome. After the complete destruction of his enemies, all of whom were Roman, Caesar staged a triumph in Rome in 45 BCE. Many Romans were opposed to such an event as Caesar's defeated foes were fellow citizens of Rome.

Caesar did show general clemency by not proscribing his enemies and instead pardoning them. This eliminated any public opposition to Caesar. Adding to his popularity were the extravagant public games and celebrations Caesar provided for the people of Rome, as well as a significant monetary gift designated in his will.

Many contemporary sources testify that Caesar used the spectacles to test the readiness of Romans to accept a monarch.

Allegedly Antony would publicly offer Caesar a crown, which he rejected. By gauging public reaction to both the offering and rejection of the crown, Caesar could judge public sentiment regarding his eventual takeover of Rome. It was evident to all that Caesar was the monarch of Rome—all but in name. Caesar needed to be particularly careful in choosing the exact moment in which to make his rule both legal and permanent.

By 46 BCE, Caesar had been Dictator for three years. He was also elected to his third and fourth terms as consul in 46 and 45 BCE respectively, serving as sole consul in his last term.

In 44 BCE, just one month before his assassination, Caesar was made Dictator in perpetuity. It now became clear that for the Republic to live, Caesar must die. On March 15, the day Caesar was meant to depart on a military campaign against the Parthian Empire, a last-minute meeting of the Roman Senate was called.

By the 1st century BCE, the Roman Senate had become so large, with more than 500 members, it was no longer meeting in the traditional Senate House. Instead, the Senate convened in the massive "Theater of Pompey" which was in the Campo

Karl von Piloty, *The Murder of Caesar*, 1865, oil on canvas, State Museum Hannover, Hannover.

de' Fiori area of modern-day Rome. Caesar's presence was, of course, a given.

Several Senators had conspired to assassinate Gaius Julius Caesar before his departure for Parthia as an act of tyrannicide. Shakespeare would of course famously recount a soothsayer warning Caesar to "beware the Ides of March" meaning the middle of the Roman month.

For March, the "Ides" would fall on the 15th day. Caesar's close ally Antony had been informed of the plot to take Caesar's life by a turncoat who had lost his nerve on the eve of the assassination. He was en route to the Senate to inform Caesar, when he was unexpectedly intercepted by other conspirators and delayed just long enough for the plan to be carried out. That day, Caesar made a mistake common among many exalted and inflated figures. Arrogance. That is, to think of oneself as untouchable, somehow existing beyond the reach of "mere mortals." That day, Caesar attended

the Senatorial meeting unarmed and without a bodyguard and he would pay for the misjudgment of this risky situation with his life.

As Caesar strode confidently into the Senate, his conspirators immediately crowded around him. When one of them swung his dagger at Caesar's neck, Caesar disbelievingly asked him "…you villain, what are you doing?"

Inspired by the aggression, the other conspirators, perhaps as many as 60 in all, leapt forward and began their savage attack on Gaius Julius Caesar, stabbing him 23 times. A later autopsy concluded that only one of the wounds had been fatal. Caesar's last words have been the stuff of historical contention for centuries.

Vincenzo Camuccini, *The Death of Julius Caesar*, 1806, oil on canvas, 112 cm x 195 cm, Galleria Nazionale d'Arte Moderna e Contemporanea, Rome.

But the words ascribed to him by Shakespeare are those that are best embedded into the collective imagination of the western world: "Et tu, Brute? Then fall, Caesar!" when he realized that Marcus Junius Brutus was among his attackers.

Brutus, Cassius and other conspirators marched through the streets of Rome chanting "People of Rome, we are once again free!" while the people locked themselves in their homes and Caesar's body lay on the stairs of the Senate for hours. A collective shock shrouded Rome over the murder of Caesar. No immediate reaction was evident.

The Romans were not certain whether to rejoice over the

death of a tyrant or protest the loss of a great ruler. Then Mark Antony read Caesar's last will and testament, claiming that Caesar had left everything to the people of Rome, effectively transforming Julius Caesar into a martyr. When Caesar's body was finally cremated, the mob began to emerge from their shock. At the sight of the body of the invincible Caesar being burned, they began singing, "He saved us only to perish at our hands," as fires were lit throughout the city.

Riots ensued. Days and days of looting, pillaging and setting buildings ablaze, a collective social catharsis took over the city. The crowd was so enraged when they discovered the two principal conspirators had fled the city, they vented their anger by killing everyone named Brutus or Cassius.

Mark Antony's Funeral Speech

"Friends, Romans, countrymen, lend me your ears;
I come to bury Caesar, not to praise him;
The evil that men do lives after them, The good is oft interred with their bones, So let it be with Caesar…
The noble Brutus hath
told you Caesar was ambitious:
If it were so, it was a grievous fault,
And grievously hath Caesar answered it… Here, under leave of Brutus and the rest, For Brutus is an honourable man;

So are they all; all honourable men
Come I to speak in Caesar's funeral…
He was my friend, faithful and just to me."

William Shakespeare
"Julius Caesar" 1539

George Edward Robertson, *Mark Antony's Oration over the Body of Caesar*, ca. 1894-1895, oil on canvas, 134 cm x 193 cm, Hartlepool Museums and Heritage Service.

Mark Antony patiently waited for the chaotic ire to subside in hopes the Romans would eventually turn to him as Caesar's logical successor. However, Caesar had designated his 19-year-old nephew, Gaius Octavian, as his legal successor.

Antony would stand by and serve as a tutor to the young Octavian and ultimately form another triumvirate: the young Octavian under the guidance of the older, more experienced Antony, and a third wealthy figure, Lepidus. After Caesar's death, these three would rule Rome as the next triumvirate.

History truly does repeat itself time and time again, and constantly reminds us that it is not easy to share power. This is a continual lesson not readily accepted by those at the top. Gradually, division began to form between the two most powerful figures, Octavian and Antony.

Antony, who had allied himself with Cleopatra in hopes of exploiting her fabulous wealth, took control of the eastern part of the empire, while Octavian ruled the western half.

Unknown artist, *Statue of Octavian Augustus*, first half of the 1st century CE, marble and bronze, 187 cm, Hermitage, St. Petersburg.

As Octavian grew older and became more experienced and even more ambitious, he realized that the coupling of Cleopatra and Mark Antony posed a danger to his own powerful yet precarious position.

Another civil war ensued, with Octavian fighting for supreme power over Rome and control of all Roman territories. This conflict came to a head in 31 BCE at the naval battle at Actium, where Octavian's general, Marcus Agrippa, definitively defeated the forces of Antony and Cleopatra, and consolidated power in the hands of Julius Caesar Octavian.

Four years later, in 27 BCE, the Roman Senate would officially declare Julius Caesar Octavian "Imperator Caesar Augustus," the first Emperor of Rome.

Despite his efforts to restore power to the Senate, it was clear that the power of Rome no longer resided in the plurality of the Senate but in the singularity of one ruler-the emperor.

Opposite: The Colosseum.

CHAPTER 3

THE COLOSSEUM

No monument better represents the grandeur and might of the Roman Empire than its largest architectural achievement—the Colosseum. The technical name for this unique structure is "amphitheater."

Amphi is the Greek word meaning "around" or "on both sides." When two theaters are joined at their open ends, the result is an amphitheater.

The official name of the Colosseum is the "Flavian Amphitheater" because it was built under the reign of three emperors, all of whom came from a single family, whose *nomen* or "clan name" was Flavia.

Construction began in 72 CE under the reign of Titus Flavius Vespasianus, better known as Vespasian. It was completed and inaugurated under the reign of his son, Titus, in 80 CE. The structure was then enlarged and the *hypogeum* or under-stage area added under the reign of Domitian, the last of the Flavian emperors.

The entirety of the Colosseum was completed within the span of a decade, an extraordinary feat considering its scale. The floor plan, or architectural footprint, is elliptical, a plane curve with two separate foci. On its longer axis, the ellipse measures

Photograph by Pajor Pawel.

189 meters (615 feet). On its shorter axis, it measures 156 meters (510 feet).

These dimensions make the Colosseum approximately equal to St. Peter's Basilica in length and as wide as Florence Cathedral is long. Yet, compared to the 120 years to complete St. Peter's and the 172 years to build Florence Cathedral, the Colosseum was finished in just eight years.

A miracle! One wonders if such a monumental structure could be completed today in such a short period of time.

That the Romans could achieve such an extraordinary feat

2,000 years ago is testimony to their immense building skills and engineering prowess.

Such accomplishments must be qualified by several historical circumstances. The first of which is that the Colosseum was the product of imperial patronage ensuring uninterrupted financial support. The second qualification is the fact that the Romans exercised forced labor, better known as "slavery." However, slaves in Rome were not just manual laborers.

Many were employed for domestic tasks and highly specialized professions such as masonry. Thus, the slaves working on the Colosseum might be as skilled as freelance masons but were

Ill. 49.—Coliseum with the Meta Sudans and a Portion of the Arch of Constantine, etching, in *History of Rome and the Popes in the Middle Ages*, by Hartmann Grisar, S.J., Paul London, 1911.

deprived of personhood and any individual rights. Slavery contributed in no small way to the incredible speed and efficiency with which the Colosseum was constructed.

The primary building material was the locally sourced travertine stone. It was quarried in Tivoli, just 32 kilometers (20 miles) outside Rome. That the Romans constructed with readily available local material is a characteristic historical feature of Italian architecture and one that was highly practical. Generally, the greatest expense for building projects is transportation.

In later Renaissance Florence, it cost ten times more to transport building materials than it did to buy materials outright. Finances were usually the driving force motivating Italian cities to build with the most available building materials.

In medieval Siena, most buildings were constructed of brick because the earth there is very rich in clay. In Florence most were constructed with dark brown sandstone called *pietraforte*.

In many ways, Italian cities are geological projections of their underlying materials.

Travertine stone, a sedimentary rock formed by the chemical precipitation of calcium carbonate minerals from fresh water, was the material used for the construction of the Colosseum, St. Peter's Basilica and many other famous Roman monuments.

Unlike Carrara marble, which is more suitable for architectural ornamentation than as a building material, Travertine is porous, giving it structural integrity, and making it a durable construction material. When the Romans quarried the Travertine, they would mark each block of stone prior to transport. Upon arrival to the building site, the workers knew exactly where each block was meant to go. The blocks were assembled one on top of another without mortar, fixed together by more than 300 tons of iron clamps. The distinct exterior of the Colosseum is entirely defined in Travertine stone with a series of three super-imposed arcades. Engaged columns partly projecting from the surface of the wall separate the semi-circular arches.

On the ground level, the order of the columns is Doric. At the middle level, they are Ionic, while at the upper level the columns are Corinthian in order.

This superimposition of all three Classical orders is one of the defining features of the Colosseum. The top level is referred to as the "attic" or low story above the cornice in a façade. By the 18th century, the term "attic" was used to refer to the space behind the highest wall of a building, which is the derivation of the modern usage of the term.

At the Colosseum, the attic was crucial to the functionality of the entire amphitheater, as its 240 mast corbels supported a retractable awning or dome known as the velarium. Architectural historians and archaeologists continue to debate over the structural nature of the velarium, specifically as to whether it covered a portion or the entire cavea, the seating area. The Latin word velarium still resonates in modern Italian as "vela," the modern Italian word for "sail." It is believed that the Romans extended a series of horizontal sails over a net-like structure made of ropes using a series of pulleys fixed to the massive wooden posts that rested on the stone corbels of the attic. Like the mechanism of sailboats, it is no surprise that the velarium was maneuvered by teams of expert sailors turning winches far below at street level to extend or retract the sails.

Jean-Léon Gérôme, *Hail Caesar! We Who Are about to Die Salute You*, 1859, oil on canvas, 93.1 x 145.4 cm, Yale University Art Gallery, New Haven.

Eighty arches define the arcade that runs along the circumference of the elliptical structure. They are marked with Roman numerals so spectators would know exactly which archway they should use to enter.

Seventy-six were used for the public, while four were used exclusively for VIPs. The designated entrance for the emperor was on the northern side, while the other axial entrances were used by Roman social elite.

Performers would access the Colosseum through underground tunnels. Modern conservative estimates put the seating capacity at approximately 50,000 people, but one ancient source claimed that as many as 87,000 people could squeeze themselves inside the amphitheater. Spectators were provided with tickets indicating their section and rows in the form of pottery shards or bone chips.

Once inside, they could access their seats through a *vomitorium* or a passageway behind or below a tier of seats that rapidly

Jean-Léon Gérôme, *The Christian Martyrs' Last Prayer*, 1860-1883, oil on canvas, 87.9 cm x 150.1 cm, Walters Art Museum, Baltimore.

dispersed spectators to and from their seats. An ancient model of the Disney method of efficiently managing crowds.

Upon entering the Colosseum today, it is difficult to make sense of what it must have been like in its heyday. Much of what is seen today is the little that is left of the original structure or is instead a reconstruction of the original architecture. For instance, the lowest area appears to be a labyrinth of brick ruins, which is what remains of the *hypogeum* underground area.

One of the major logistical disadvantages of an amphitheater is that there is no place for a backstage. For a theatrical event to run properly, a backstage area-used for dressing rooms, theatrical machinery, scenery and props storage-is essential. The Romans solved this problem by building an "under stage" that today appears as a pit-like space at the center of the ellipse, inside of which are a series of curvilinear walls.

The entire hypogeum was covered by a wooden platform, which was in turn covered with sand, the Latin word for which is *harenae* or arena, from which the modern usage of the word "arena" is derived. When a Roman said that the gladiators were fighting in the arena, he was being quite literal as the gladiators were fighting on the sands of the Colosseum.

The performance area was surrounded by a four-meters-high (13 feet) brick wall known as the podium. Much like modern sports fans who want to sit close to the event to feel like part of the action, so too did the Romans. However, being so close to the action in the Colosseum was also putting oneself in peril. At only four meters in height, a contest involving a tiger or an elephant-which could easily clear such a height- would place the audience in immediate danger. Spectators were protected by safety devices like upturned elephant tusks positioned around the circumference. Should an animal try to escape the pit, it would either injure or kill itself in the process.

The seating area-or *cavea*-is one of the most difficult things to understand inside the Colosseum today. Originally, the interior part was white in color because the entire structure was dressed in white marble assembled into rows of seats.

Co-centric tiered rows defined the entire interior circumference of the ellipse, row upon row upon row of seats, on an incline from the very bottom to the very top, broken up into four distinct sections. Where one sat was a direct reflection of one's social status. Similar to European or American football games today where the "best seats in the house" are those by the 50-yard line, the Colosseum's imperial box was also located "at the 50-yard line" on the north side of the ellipse, while on the opposite side there was a special box reserved for the Vestal Virgins.

Reconstructed seating inside the Colosseum.

Surrounding them at the lowest podium level were the Senators. The next tier up was occupied by the non-senatorial noble class known as the *maenianums primum.*

Above them sat ordinary Roman citizens, the *plebians,* in the *maenianum secundum.* Those seats highest up and furthest away were reserved for women and the common poor in the *maenianum secundum in legneis.*

Amazingly, when you are inside the great amphitheater today, you can still appreciate that taking place inside the Colosseum was, of course...the stuff of legend.

Opposite: Remains of the Hypogeum.
Photograph by Pamela Lico.

Opposite: Paris Bordone, *Gladiator Camp*, ca. 1560, oil on canvas, 218 cm x 329 cm, Kunsthistorisches Museum, Vienna.

CHAPTER 4

BLOOD SPORT

If you were to visit the Colosseum 2,000 years ago on an event day, it would look very similar to a football or baseball stadium today. Contemporary Roman chroniclers tell us different people arrived at the Colosseum at specific times. When the spectators entered the Colosseum, they were greeted by performances whose intensity gradually increased throughout the day.

The earliest performances involved tamed animal tricks like dancing bears and tigers leaping through hoops of fire. As more people gradually filled the arena, another spectacle would begin. One that was introduced by the emperor Nero in an earlier amphitheater but was later performed in the Colosseum was a comedy act of sorts. A non-mortal combat with women dressed as gladiators fighting dwarves dressed as gladiators. Ancient Roman humor!

When this spectacle ended, the following event involved animal combat. Animals that had no possibility of meeting each other in nature would be forced to fight one another to the death in the arena.

The far-flung borders of the empire made it easy for the Romans to capture all sorts of exotic animals that would

The Great Hunt, ca. 320 CE, mosaic, floor from the villa at Piazza Amerina, Sicily.

otherwise never have crossed paths if not for the purpose of entertaining the blood-thirsty interests of the Romans.

After the animals were captured in the wild, they were starved, taunted and provoked so that by the time they were released into the arena, they were foaming at the mouth and agitated into an explosive performance of survival of the fittest. Numerous animals would be fighting at one time-a tiger versus a lion, a bear versus a pack of hyenas. But there would also be more docile animals such as cows scattered throughout the performance space.

These large slow-moving animals would often fall victim to the wild and random charges of rhinoceroses, which were habitual performers. One Roman chronicler describes precisely what happened when a fully accelerated charging rhinoceros slammed into the side of cow:

"The initial explosion of the cow whose remaining carcass would go careening into the stands and whose blood would send the other animals into a frenzy, inciting a full-out melee." For ancient Romans, this spectacle was especially fascinating. Not only were they seeing many animals for the first time (imagine what it must have been like for a Roman to first lay eyes upon a giraffe, alligator or a hippopotamus) they also got to watch these animals viciously rip each other to pieces.

Once the animal contests concluded, attendants would come out to carry off the animal carcasses and turn over the sand. Sand was a particularly efficient material with which to cover the wooden platform of the Colosseum. All that needed to be done to hide the blood, guts and gored flesh was to simply turn it over. If the sand could no longer absorb organic matter, attendants would clear it out and bring in fresh sand to replenish the arena.

The next event, known as the *venatio*, drew much attention and occupied most of the morning agenda. The venatio involved a performer known as a *"bestiarius"*–or a professional beast hunter. The essential appeal of venatio contests was that it became a close-up vicarious experience spectators could enjoy from the safety of their seats without putting themselves in harm's way.

A *bestiarius* would dress and arm himself the same way he would were he out in the jungle or on the plains of the Serengeti to put his extraordinary skills on display.

Props and scenery were also used to recreate the actual terrain and setting of various far-off places

Zilten Mosaic, 2nd century CE, mosaic, 573 cm x 397 cm, The Archaeological Museum of Tripoli, Tripoli.

Big Game Hunt, ca. 320 CE, mosaic, floor from the villa at Piazza Amerina, Sicily. Photograph © José Luiz Bernardes Ribeiro / CC BY-SA 4.0.

to provide the audience with an authentic virtual experience of the hunt.

The *bestiarii* would march out into the arena; the trapdoors of the Colosseum would spring open and dozens upon dozens of lions, tigers and cheetahs would burst forth—and the hunt was on! It was a contest between hunter and beast. Spectators typically cheered on the hunter, but if a particular animal performed quite well, they might root for the animal instead. The hunt would continue until either most or all the animals had died or were incapacitated. Once the contest had come to an end, attendants would clear off both human and animal carcasses alike in preparation for the next event.

The preferred animal of slaughter in the Colosseum was the elephant, most likely because its enormous size made it such a spectacular animal to take down. There is a legend concerning opening day at the Colosseum in 80 CE, when 5,000 animals were allegedly killed. Logistically, such a feat would be nearly impossible because it would result in three and half beasts being killed per minute. More than likely, the 5,000 animals were killed over the first 100 days of inaugural games at the Colosseum. In either case, it is both a staggering and frightening figure.

One of the most gruesome stories regarding the Colosseum happened in the recent past. The Colosseum metro stop is located just across the street from the amphitheater and was constructed in the mid-20th century. Allegedly, as the workers were digging the underground metro tunnel past the Colosseum, they came across a mass grave of elephants.

Presumably, on a particular day, a vast number of elephants had been slaughtered and their carcasses dragged nearby and interred in a mass grave. When this mass grave was rediscovered by workers nearly 2,000 years later, they discovered that because so many carcasses had been packed into the space, those located at the bottom still had rotting flesh attached to the bones—a disturbing example of disregard for humane treatment of animals in antiquity.

Typically, there was an intermission in the spectacles after the

beast hunts. If spectators lived close by, they could go home and have something to eat, perhaps even take a nap.

If one did not live nearby, there were plenty of concession stands, known as a *popina*, outside the Colosseum serving everything from hotdogs (sausages) and stews to alcoholic beverages such as mead and spiced wine.

In the afternoon, the crowds would usually arrive well before the spectacle began. This is because the afternoon program was what everyone wanted to see: the gladiatorial contests-fights to the death between highly trained combatants. The spectators would be beside themselves with anticipation—pounding their feet, chanting wildly, waiting for the gladiators to emerge. Just as the crowd was about to become unhinged, trumpets would sound and the gladiators entered the performance area. They marched once around the entirety of the arena to the crowd's screams and applause.

Gladiators were authentic celebrities in their day. Similar to today's music concerts when fans become emotionally overwhelmed at the sight of their idols, so too, did ancient Romans react in the presence of a famous gladiator. Fighting in the

The Ludwig Boltzmann Institute for Archaeological Prospection and Virtual Archaeology.

Studio artist of Firmin Didot, *Gladiators Fighting Barbary Lion*.

Colosseum was the equivalent of singing in Madison Square Garden or performing at halftime during the Superbowl. It was the mecca of the gladiatorial profession, the largest and most distinguished amphitheater in the Roman world. The combatants were usually slaves, prisoners of war or criminals. At gladiator schools, called *ludi gladatorium,* they would be trained to fight in a specific way with distinct armament.

A *murmillo* gladiator was armed with a gladius sword, a two- and one-half foot long sword from which gladiators got their name, and an oblong shield like those carried by legionaries. A *retiarius* gladiator would be trained to use a long trident and a

Jean-Léon Gérôme, *Pollice Verso*, 1872, oil on canvas, 96.5 cm x 149.2 cm, Phoenix Art Museum, Phoenix.

net. A *hoplomachus* gladiator would fight with a long spear and small circular shield.

Certain gladiator types were traditionally matched against each other—*murmillo vs. Thracian or hoplomaches; retiarius vs. secutores or murmillo.*

Gladiators were all trained in a specific martial art and would fight each other to the death. "Blood sport" was what the Romans called it. A "knockout" in these gladiatorial contests was most likely fatal. There was an "out" at the fatal hour. If a gladiator was incapacitated by injury, he could throw himself at the mercy of the emperor or the next highest-ranking person in attendance. The way a gladiator did this was by simply falling to his knees

Unknown artist, *A Roman Holiday*, in *The Illustrated History of the World, for the English People. From the Earliest Period to the Present Time, Ancient—Medieval—Modern. With Many Original High-Class Engravings* by Ward, Lock, & Co., Warwick House, London, 1881-1884.

and extending his index and middle fingers to indicate that he was yielding or submitting. It was up to the emperor, the Vestal Virgins or a senator to exercise the power of life or death.

The emperor's decision was communicated through a thumb-based gesture, *pollice verso*, although there is some controversy concerning exactly what this gesture was. Popular culture has immortalized the gesture as a thumbs up, meaning "let him live" or a thumbs down, meaning "execute him." While certain archaeologists suggest that the gesture involved a thumb extended laterally. Most recently, it has been proposed that the gesture always involved a laterally extended thumb and that the gesture indicating life or death was an open or closed hand.

Crowd sentiment and reaction heavily influenced the emperor's decision. If the gladiator had fought valiantly enough, he might have been granted the opportunity to live and fight another day; if not, he would meet his end. However, there was

no confusing the words that accompanied the decision: *Mitte!*–"Let him live" or *Lugula!*–"Kill him!"

As the defeated gladiator took his last gasp of breath, the winning gladiator would take a victory lap, accolades and applause pouring down upon him, standing amongst tens of thousands of people chanting his name at the center of what was then the entire world-*the caput mundi*. Adrenaline pumping through his veins as he came to the realization that he had lived to fight another day-a day which might, very likely, be his last.

Curiously, the enormous popularity of the gladiatorial games was reflective of the decay of Roman society during its imperial period. In other words, the Roman spectators sitting in the stands of the Colosseum were once the very Roman soldiers who had made Rome so powerful. In distant battlefields, they once fought for the glory of Rome. But Rome had become so large and powerful that most of its soldiers were now conquered subjects to whom citizenship had been granted. While these new Romans were sent to distant fronts, those citizens who lived in Rome itself were sitting apathetically in the stands of the Colosseum and fighting vicariously through the contests taking place in front of them. The Colosseum became a cultural black hole, gradually overshadowing all other forms of art, sport and entertainment.

Just a mile west of the Colosseum is the famous Theatre of Marcellus, built in the 1st century BCE under Julius Caesar. Still today, the Theatre of Marcellus is the world's largest theater with a capacity of upwards of 10,000 people.

Night after night, fewer and fewer Romans would frequent the Theater of Marcellus, as theatre gradually lost its appeal. Romans no longer wanted to experience thought-provoking and inspirational theatrical performances. What they now preferred was an immediate experience of spectacular and gratuitous violence, and that is what they received at the Colosseum.

In a desperate attempt to fill its seats, the producers at the Theatre of Marcellus tried to play to the public's taste for blood by introducing what today we call a "double." That is, if the screenplay of a theatrical performance called for the protagonist or antagonist to die, the actor would be substituted by a slave who was killed during the performance. Yet, it seems that even this extreme act was not enough to bring the crowds back to theatre. What the public wanted was not outright killing, but "blood sport" instead.

The only place to get that was...inside the Colosseum.

Opposite: Thomas Couture, *The Romans in Their Decadence*, 1847, oil on canvas, 472 cm x 772 cm, Musée d'Orsay, Paris.

CHAPTER 5

BREAD & CIRCUS

Just as Shakespearean times had its "salad days" and the 1960s had its "days of wine and roses," ancient Romans relished their "bread and circus" era. It was a most decadent period when emperors provided both lavish foods and spectacular entertainment to keep the citizens contented and non-controversial. In Latin, it is known as the period of *panem et circenses*.

The magnificent Colosseum had been completed in the last couple of decades of the 1st century CE, at which point Rome was nearing its zenith of greatest territorial expansion. It was under the reign of Emperor Trajan (c. 100 CE) that the Roman Empire would reach its furthest limits and blood sport had reached its peak of popularity.

The power and wealth of Rome was reflected in the urban reality of its capital, Rome itself. At the time of Trajan, the greater urban population of Rome numbered about one million people. This may not seem that impressive today compared to Asian cities like Shanghai, but in the ancient world, this figure was staggering. Rome was the second largest city in the Western world after Alexandria in Egypt.

Very few other large cities existed at that time. Most people still lived in rural or provincial countryside settings.

Furthermore, of the million-plus people who inhabited Rome, 650,000 of them were on the public dole—or welfare. The Roman state was so wealthy it could afford to support two out of every three of its citizens.

This welfare was not, by any means, Campbell's soup and Ramen noodles. During this heyday, Romans were dining on the equivalent of Beluga caviar while sipping champagne. This wasn't charity. Providing its citizens with rich foods was a show of wealth and prosperity. But, as one historian put it, "a bored people is one that is ripe for revolution." Yes, you must not only keep their bellies full, you must also keep the Roman mind occupied to distract it from the collective apathy, or civic boredom, that was brewing.

One of the key subliminal messages of the gladiatorial contests on display inside the Colosseum was that the average Roman was now living vicariously through the gladiator. Up until the

Auguste Leloir, *Horace at Tibur*, in *The Literature of All Nations and All Ages; History, Character, and Incident* by Julian Hawthorne, John Russell Young, and John Porter Lamberton, Chicago, IL, 1900.

Alexey Tarasovich Markov, *Saint Eustace in the Colosseum*, 1839, oil on canvas, 98 cm x 136.5 cm, State Tretyakov Gallery, Moscow.

time of Christ, it was the Roman himself out on the battlefield fighting for home and country. Now, it was the gladiator fighting for the common citizen. The gladiatorial contests were a means to divert civic boredom. It became a way for Romans to express their support and passion for their country without having to go to battle themselves.

Hence, the era of "bread and circus." Bread, because the Roman state was actually feeding its population, and circus, because the state was also providing entertainment, or spectacle, to keep Roman minds off collective boredom. Not surprisingly, it was during the era of bread and circus that gladiatorial contests reached their peak of popularity

What exactly were gladiatorial contests and where did they come from? Like much of ancient Roman culture, the gladiatorial contests were borrowed, or inherited, from the ancient Etruscan civilization. When a distinguished Etruscan male patriarch died, the funeral was accompanied by games. Slaves owned by the deceased patriarch were forced to fight to the death in his honor. Slaves who gave up their lives was not only reflective of the importance of the deceased, but also meant that those who died during the fight would accompany the patriarch into the afterlife. It was from this tradition, referred to as *munus* (which translates as human sacrifice-plural *munera*), from which the gladiatorial contests were derived.

However, in the 1st century BCE, when Rome was still a republic, the law limited the number of gladiatorial games to one per year in the Roman provinces. In the capital of Rome proper, it was limited to two gladiatorial contests a year. One in the provinces; two in Rome.

This was the rule until Rome was transformed into an empire. Blood sport became the most effective means by which emperors could gain popularity, a sure-fire political maneuver. If you're the

Unknown artist, *Retiarius vs secutor from Borghese mosaic*, ca. 320 CE, mosaic, Villa Borghese, Rome.

emperor, and your predecessor put on five games, you're going to offer ten. Under the reign of Rome's first emperor, Augustus, legislation was still limiting the number or gladiatorial contests to two per year. However, five more per year were permitted in honor of the emperor himself, and on top of that, five more in honor of the emperor's family and children-totaling twelve per year.

Following Augustus, each succeeding emperor added on another five under his reign, resulting in the exponential growth of the number of days upon which gladiatorial games could be staged in Rome.

The number of contests permitted exploded into a staggering figure. Of those 365 1/4 days of the Julian Calendar (Roman solar year), 93 days were public holidays, which were celebrated with games. The contests became a way to celebrate, much like a parade for Thanksgiving or Columbus Day, or bowls for football games.

Gladiatorial games in the Colosseum assumed the prestigious role of public expression for the importance of a specific holiday.

On top of that, there were 39 non-coinciding religious holidays. Furthermore, there were an additional 30 imperial holidays celebrating the emperor and his family, all of which were celebrated with gladiatorial games. When the numbers are tabulated, it totals 162 days being celebrated with games—nearly the equivalent of an entire school year. No society in history had more time off than ancient Rome, not even modern-day France! Naturally, the Romans were consumed by the goings-on in the Colosseum.

In many ways, the Colosseum, as spectacular as it is, represented the rotting core of a decadent Roman society that was becoming quite fat and lazy. The building of the Colosseum, however, would not mark the end of the creation of some of the most spectacular engineering and architectural feats in history.

Only a few decades later, during the reign of Emperor Hadrian, Rome witnessed the construction of the greatest of its temples—the Pantheon.

Opposite: Interior of the Pantheon. Photograph by Khorzhevska.

CHAPTER 6

THE PANTHEON

The Pantheon has been described as the most perfect architectural monument ever created. As the author of this book, I am in total agreement with that assessment.

The name—"Pantheon"—describes the building's function. In Greek, *Pan* means "all" and *theon* means "god." Therefore, the Pantheon is a temple dedicated, collectively, to all gods. This makes the Pantheon especially unique, considering that most of the temples in Rome are dedicated to a specific god or goddess. For instance, the Temple of Saturn or the Temple of Juno. The Pantheon, instead, is dedicated to all the Roman deities.

Construction took place over a seven-year period, from 118 until 125 CE. Although the structure is not nearly as large as the Colosseum, the fact that the Romans were able to build it in less than a decade is still a remarkable accomplishment, especially considering the complexity of the construction of the perfect hemispherical dome, which is an engineering masterpiece.

The Pantheon was erected under the reign of the enlightened emperor Hadrian, the successor to the celebrated military emperor Trajan, who expanded the Roman Empire to its greatest point of territorial breadth. Emperor Hadrian happened to fall

Facade of the Pantheon.

into the most fortunate position of reaping the benefits of Trajan's era of conquest.

Hadrian's goal as emperor was to visit the four corners of his empire, to see the entirety of the vast territory under his control. It was also under Hadrian that some of Rome's greatest monuments were erected. The remains of Hadrian's Villa in Tivoli just outside Rome is still a spectacle—the grounds are studded with fountains, temples and exquisite statues. However, the monument that most embodies Hadrian's exalted reign is the Pantheon.

Hadrian wisely employed a Greek architect, Apollodorous, to design the Pantheon. This fact is often a cause for confusion because one can still see the inscription on the porch of the Pantheon which indicates otherwise.

A large bronze-lettered inscription reads:

M. AGRIPPA. L. F. COS TERTIUM. FECIT.

- "M. Agrippa" stands for "Marcus Agrippa" (the admiral who won the empire for Augusts in 31 BCE at the Battle of Actium)
- "L" is the first letter of Agrippa's father's name—Lucius.
- "F" is the first letter of the Latin word "filius" which, together, means "son of Lucius" and therefore, "Marcus Agrippa, Son of Lucius"
- 'C-O-S' stands for consul, which was the prime minister's position. (There were always two consuls to check and balance power.)
- "Tertium" translates as "thrice"
- "Fecit" means "had this built"

The full inscription translates as: "Marcus Agrippa, Son of Lucius, consul for the third time, built this." This inscription does not refer to the Pantheon that we see today, but rather to an earlier temple that once stood in its place. The dedication was simply carried over. Marcus Agrippa had nothing at all to do with the Hadrianic construction of the Pantheon, though he was the patron of the original structure that stood on the same site.

When a modern visitor happens on the Pantheon today, the experience is very different from what it would have been like two millennia ago. Now, a visitor can walk right through the front door into the massive dome-covered space. When it was first built though, there was a large rectangular courtyard surrounded by colonnades or porticoes, on all four sides. The technical name for this large courtyard was *quadriporticus* or "four porticoes." The longer sides were parallel to the Pantheon and the shorter sides perpendicular to the structure.

One of those four sides is the actual porch itself of the Pantheon. One needs only to look at a map of Rome to see the

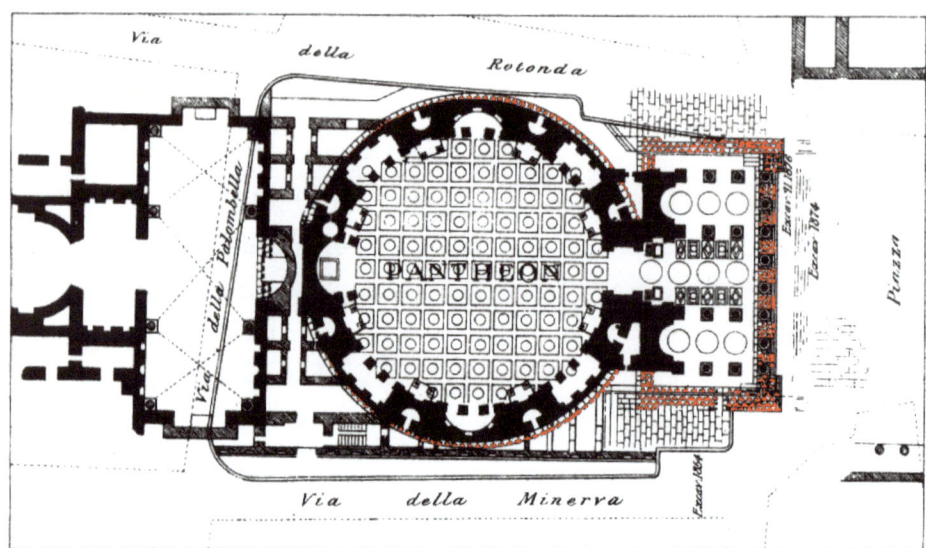

Plan of the First (Red) and of the Third (Black) Pantheon, in *The Ruins and Excavations of Ancient Rome*, by R. Lanciani, 1897.

outline of that quadriporticus still present in the urbanism of Rome today.

The piazza in front of the Pantheon, the Piazza della Rotonda, still has the distinct rectangular shape of the quadriporticus.

Thus, you had to first walk all the way around and through a door on one of the short sides of the rectangular quadriporticus to enter.

Once inside, you would be met with a mini triumphal arch in the center of the quadriporticus. Eventually you would make your way up to the actual porch of the Pantheon itself, which was initially the fourth side of the quadriporticus.

Today only one porch stair is visible although originally there were many more. Over time, ancient Rome has gradually begun to sink into the ground. As recently as the late 1990s, there were five stairs still visible leading into the Pantheon. At that time, the area in front had a stagnated water problem and in recent decades, the level of the piazza has been raised so that only one remaining stair is visible.

Looking to the sides of the Pantheon, you will get a very clear idea of just how much Rome has risen over 2,000 years and just how much these ancient monuments have sunk. The stairs represent a sacred separation between mortals and the gods, as well as being a significant architectural feature. All ancient Roman and Etruscan temples were uplifted onto podium bases. They were raised above the ground to demonstrate how important these structures were, and were also used to ascend to the temple proper.

The porch of the Pantheon consists of sixteen 40-Roman-foot-tall (39 feet) monolithic Egyptian granite columns. Sixteen is MANY; 40-Roman feet-tall means VERY LARGE. "Monolithic" translates to columns made from a SINGLE shaft of stone. It

Jean-Claude Golvin, *Hadrian's Pantheon*, 2000, ink, gouache, and watercolor on paper, 31.1 cm x 37.8 cm, private collection.

Top: Emanuel Brune, *Detail from Temple of Mars Vengeur, Rome*, in *Cyclopedia of Architecture, Carpentry, and Building* by various authors, 2009.

was impressive craftsmanship for masons working with crude tools and awkward moving devices.

The cylindrical part of the column itself is a single piece of granite, one of the heaviest substances on earth, imported directly from Egypt.

Just moving the material to Rome was an amazing undertaking, but then raising the columns to create the porch was extraordinary. When one passes, rubbing your hand over them provides a sense of the sheer mass of the object.

It takes three or four people holding hands to wrap around the circumference of a single column.

The columns of the porch are surmounted by a pediment, the triangular upper part of the building and a typical element of all Greek and Roman temples. The pediment and the actual triangular tympanum, or the flat space inside the triangle,

once contained a large bronze sculptural relief of an eagle. The body of the eagle was upright, filling the vertical space at the center and its outstretched wings occupying the narrow spaces on the sides. The holes which once fixed the bronze sculpture to the pediment itself are still visible today.

The eagle is no longer there because it was ripped out in the 1620s under the reign of Pope Urban VIII (Maffeo Barberini). Not in warfare or revenge, but because of economics. It was removed so the bronze could be melted down and incorporated into the 96 tons of bronze required to build Gian Lorenzo Bernini's massive and impressive 10-story *Baldacchino* in St. Peter's Basilica.

The practice of looting and then repurposing materials led to a famous saying in Rome: "That which the barbarians did not do, the Barberini did," meaning that whatever the barbarians didn't steal or destroy in ancient times was pillaged by the Barberini family in the Renaissance when one in their ranks became pope. In all fairness to the Barberini family, it was not an uncommon practice for Christian popes to loot ancient pagan monuments.

Back to the quadriporticus…whose purpose was to build suspense, disguising the mystery of what lay within. The interior of the Pantheon is perhaps the most singular space on earth. Stepping inside the Pantheon is walking into a perfect form—the symbolic representation of infinity.

Successful architecture is the harmonious and proportional division of space, and no structure embodies that harmonious division of space better than the Pantheon. It is a unique and spectacular contribution to architectural history.

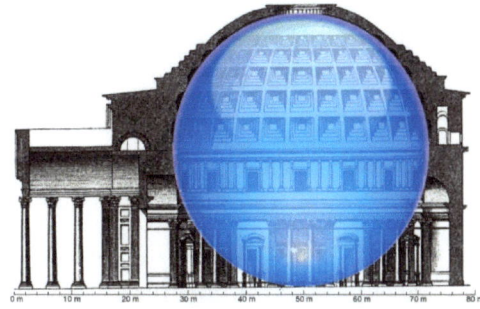

Right: Derivative work: Cmglee, CC BY-SA 3.0, via Wikimedia Commons.

The floor plan, or the architectural footprint of the Pantheon, is circular with a width of exactly 43 meters (142 feet.) If cut in half vertically to create what is called its section, it is a hemispherical dome. At the top of that dome, a tape measure dropped to the bottom would reveal that the height is also exactly 43 meters (142 feet.) Thus, the Pantheon is in a perfect one-to-one vertical-to-horizontal proportion. The interior space one enters is nothing less than a perfect sphere—the representation of eternity.

In architecture, there is a concrete concept of harmony between repeating spaces and solids. Reading the ground plan, a pattern begins to unfold of a perfect balance of solids and voids proceeding all the way around. A frequent question is: "Why is the Pantheon in such great shape today? How has it held up so well over two millennia?"

Part of the answer is because in 607 CE, it was named "Santa Maria ad Martyres." Because it was consecrated as a sacred Christian site, it fell under the protection of the church. In theory, one could not loot the Pantheon, with, of course, the exception of Baroque popes.

The altar of the Pantheon is a Christian altar. In pagan times, there would have been an altar as well because temples were used for sacrifice, although in ancient Roman times, sacrifice was typically performed outdoors, not inside the temple proper.

The arch above the altar and opposite it, above the entrance, is the same semicircular arch.

Again, perfect symmetry.

Sitting at the middle level is the drum, an architectural section that negotiates the dome onto the base of the structure proper.

One section looks quite different from the rest. That piece is a reconstruction of the original decorative scheme of the Pantheon. It is rather busy. In fact, it might even be considered tacky. The decoration consists of polychrome marble, a white marble screen and recesses or windows.

It is important to note that this is because the inside of the Pantheon today is 18th-century Baroque decoration, which, surprisingly, is not very different from what it originally looked like back in the year 125 CE. We have this concept that ancient Greek and Roman architecture was very minimalist. We imagine the Parthenon in Athens, the Pantheon or the Colosseum as looking like a Calvin Klein-esque commercial. Everything very simple, austere and severe in design. This is a complete misconception. What we see today are the stony gray remains of a what was once a brightly painted décor. Lots of vivid color!

By modern standards, the Romans and Greeks were extremely gaudy in their decorative tastes. They loved to polychrome. The Parthenon in Athens was originally painted, though the paint has chipped away and fallen off over the years. Not only was the Parthenon painted, it looked like a big Lifesaver candy wrapper, with bright yellows, light blues and vibrant pinks. The same goes for the Roman Pantheon. In many ways, the Baroque interior today is reflective of what the original interior decoration would have looked like two millennia ago. Think of the Metropolitan Museum's 2022-2023 exhibit "Chroma: Ancient Sculpture in Color," which examined the wild polychromy of ancient art we all thought was the dreary gray we see today. Like the fall of the Roman Empire, the polychromy eventually flaked off and faded away over time.

Structurally, the drum holds up the hemispherical coffered dome overhead, which is considered the most perfect of all architectural forms. If architecture is supposed to be the harmonious

balance between space and solids, then no structure does so more successfully than a hemispherical coffered dome.

First, because the dome itself is a perfect balance of concave and convex forms that contain space, while also projecting out into the infinite space of the sky that surrounds it.

Second, because each coffer does, on a micro level, what the dome does on a macro level. Each coffer acts like a mini-dome, puncturing the shell of the dome itself.

It is very aesthetically pleasing to walk inside the Pantheon—a vast space covered by a single membrane dome. What few realize is how difficult it truly is to build such a perfect structure.

The Pantheon is the mother of all domes. The father of all domes, for this author, is Brunelleschi's dome in the city of Florence built in the 15th century. But the Pantheon is more of an engineering marvel. That the Romans could have built such a complex structure in 118 CE is mind-boggling. How did they conceive and build such a dome? What allowed them to do it was a specific technology that disappeared for the entire medieval and

Renaissance period. That technology was the ingenious use of a mundane compound material-poured concrete.

The concrete used by the Romans consisted of a formula of lime, sand, water and pozzolana (volcanic ash taken from Mt. Vesuvius) which acted as an accelerator so the drying process was a chemical reaction between the components. It was not evaporation. This type of concrete could actually dry underwater. The Roman builders poured successive rings of the concrete mixture into massive wooden molds to construct the dome. While it is very simple to describe the process, structurally speaking, it's rather complicated.

As the dome rises, it must get thinner to reduce its weight. From the outside, the Pantheon does not have the distinct curvilinear shape that domes typically do. Instead, it is stepped and looks like a series of concentric rings with edges and clear vertical planes moving up. It was designed this way to contain the outward thrust produced by all domes known as "hoop stress." But the steps are not a separate feature from the shell.

Their shape is inherent in the mold used when the concrete was poured. The lower portion of the dome is thicker and reinforced. Pieces of Travertine stone were tossed into the concrete

to make it stronger. But since every successive pour was thinner than the previous, the weight of the aggregate was also reduced. For instance, bricks and pottery fragments were used in the middle to upper areas of the dome.

The smooth area around the oculus—the opening—is the thinnest point, where the Romans used pumice stone as aggregate, a very hard resilient stone. A piece of pumice thrown into water will float.

The diameter of the oculus is exactly 30 feet across, which is one-fourth the total diameter of the dome. The oculus thus functions as a compression ring. If it were any larger, the dome would look unfinished, but if it were any smaller, the dome would collapse, because the oculus serves the same function as a keystone in an arch. The structure is fighting against gravity.

By definition, a dome is nothing more than an arch rotated 360 degrees in space. The hemispherical dome, which in section is a semicircular arch, is pulled down by gravity at its peak in a bending downward movement, meaning that all the thrust is lateral. It is literally pushing out sideways. This is called, as mentioned earlier, "hoop stress."

The external steps on the Pantheon function like the rings around a wine barrel to stay the outward thrust of the dome proper. Instead of pulling down on the keystone, gravity pulls down on the entire circumference of the oculus, the 30-foot diameter opening at the top of the dome that locks the dome in place. This is engineering mastery at its most brilliant.

The science of statics as we know it today was not invented until the 19th century. Compression strength, tensile strength-none of these principles were known until nearly a millennium after the Pantheon was built. Yet, somehow, the Romans were able to estimate these various concepts in constructing the Pantheon nearly 2,000 years ago.

The fact that the oculus is open is indicative that ancient

Greek and Roman classical architecture was not meant to alienate nature. It aims to integrate nature. This isn't Frederick Law Olmsted's vision of Central Park, where every blade of grass is contained within a rectangular perimeter. Here, nature is invited inside; it is meant to become part of the architecture itself. If you're ever in Rome and it's raining, don't walk, run to the Pantheon to see one of the most enchanting sights in the world: rain coming in through the oculus. Regardless of how windy or hard it's raining, the raindrops always fall through the oculus in a perfect cylinder.

If you look at the floors below the oculus, you'll see ornate drain holes in certain areas to catch the rainfall.

So yes, it rains inside the Pantheon.

It rarely snows in Rome, but when it does, it snows inside the Pantheon as well. Natural light also filters through the oculus in dramatic ways. On April 21, which tradition maintains is the birthday of Rome, the sun falls through the screen above the main door and floods the porch!

For this reason, it has been surmised that the Pantheon was perhaps a type of sundial. Since all the Roman gods are associated with different times of the year, the beam of light would hit particular representations of the gods, depending on the season.

Today, the statues and paintings inside of the Pantheon are all Christian in subject, but originally, they were all pagan—Venus, Mars and Mercury. If it was springtime, the season of Venus, the light would filter through the oculus and fall on her statue.

No one knows for certain how exactly the Pantheon functioned as a sundial, but the fact remains that the Pantheon continues to evoke incredible mysticism, mystery and spirituality.

CHAPTER 7

CONSTANTINE & CHRISTIANITY

To fully appreciate Emperor Constantine's world-changing role in the rise of Christianity in the 4th century CE, take a close look at the monument adjacent the Colosseum, a hallmark in architectural history.

The Arch of Constantine is one of only three triumphal arches still standing in Rome. They served as resplendent trophies celebrating an important military victory on the part of a general or emperor.

The most famous of them all is the Arch of Titus, built around 80 CE in the Forum to celebrate Emperor Titus's victory over Jerusalem. At the other end of the Forum is the Arch of Septimius Severus, father of the infamous emperor Caracalla, dedicated in 203 CE. However, the monument that remains the most influential and revolutionary is the Arch of Constantine.

It was erected to commemorate Constantine's victory over the previous incumbent, Maxentius in 312 CE. By the late 3rd century CE, the Roman Empire had become so large it had been divided into four sections. There were two Augustuses and two Caesars, totaling four rulers, known as the Tetrachy, over the entirety of the Roman Empire.

Having multiple rulers naturally led to infighting. The emperors

Piero della Francesca, *Constantine's Dream*, ca. 1466, fresco, 329 cm x 190 cm, San Francesco, Arezzo.

fought among themselves for absolute supremacy as each wanted to rule the whole Roman territory. This infighting led to Constantine's eventual takeover when he overthrew Maxentius.

As Christian legend tells the story, the night before Constantine's attack, he had a dream in which an angel revealed to him a crucifix and spoke these destiny-inspired words: "In this sign, thou shall conquer," referring to the cross. After his prophetic dream, Constantine instructed all his soldiers to draw the symbol of the cross on their shields before leading them into battle against Emperor Maxentius.

The battle ensued in 312 CE at Rome's Milvian Bridge. Constantine's troops were overwhelmed by the size of his opponent's army. Yet somehow Constantine emerged victorious.

According to legend, Maxentius fell to his death from the bridge just as their armies were amassing on a narrow passage point. Maxentius' heavy metal armor caused him to drown in the Tiber River.

Following Maxentius' death, Constantine rose to power as the sole emperor of the Western Empire. Constantine always maintained that it was the Christian symbol of the cross that

Raphael, *The Battle at Pons Milvius,* 1520, fresco, Palazzo Apostolico, Vatican.

had granted him this victory. One year later, Constantine ratified legislation known as the Edict of Milan, a religious tolerance act allowing all religions being practiced on Roman soil to be recognized. One of those religions was Christianity and thus began its swift rise.

What if the circumstances had been different? Imagine if Constantine had lost the battle at the Milvian Bridge and had not ratified the Edict of Milan. What would the world look like today?

Constantine's victory remains one of the most critical moments in world history; it was this event that propelled Christianity to the forefront of western civilization as the religion grafting itself onto the very fabric of the Roman Empire. About two decades later, Constantine abruptly moved the capital from Rome to a city crafted from scratch and named after himself, Constantinople, which is modern-day Istanbul, Turkey, a distance of 1,374 kilometres (854 miles) from Rome. Constantine relocated the epicenter of Roman territory from the extreme west to the very center of the empire. When Constantine made this radical political move, it left a significant power vacuum in the western part of the empire. Without the physical presence of an emperor, the west found itself in a vulnerable position. Wherever the emperor and his imperial court were located was where the center of power resided. Not surprisingly, within a century or so, numerous incursions and uprisings erupted in the western territories. The empire was ripe for invasion.

Constantine began publicly advocating for Christianity, even though he wasn't baptized until he was on his deathbed. Scholars argue whether Constantine himself can be considered a true Christian, though it is known for certain that Constantine's mother, Saint Helena, was indeed a Christian. Saint Helena is recognized as a saint for two reasons:

Paolo Veronese, *The Dream of Saint Helena*, ca. 1570, oil on canvas, 197.5 cm x 115.6 cm, The National Gallery, London.

1. It is believed that she was largely responsible for convincing her son to make Christianity the religion of the Roman Empire and

2. She took it upon herself to return to the Holy Land to look for the true cross upon which Jesus was crucified.

When Saint Helena arrived in the Holy Land nearly 300 years after the crucifixion of Christ, the whereabouts of the actual cross had fallen into obscurity. Helena began looking into where the cross could be found. She finally discovered a man (coincidentally named

Judas) who knew of its location. But Judas stubbornly refused to disclose the site to her. Helena resorted to a very un-Christian means to convince him to tell her where the cross was. She dropped him into a well and starved him until he revealed its whereabouts.

This coercive tactic worked and he took her to a site where they began digging. To their surprise, they found not one but three crosses because according to the Gospels, Christ was crucified in the company of the so-called "good" and "bad" thieves.

Helena had to determine which of the three crosses was the true Holy Cross. Just as she was contemplating them, a funeral procession came marching by. She decided to take the three crosses and lower them one by one over the deceased. With the first cross, nothing happened. Again, with the second cross, nothing happened. Finally, with the third, the deceased person miraculously came back to life. Therefore, Helena determined that the third cross was the one upon which Jesus must have been crucified. Today, in the Church of the Holy Sepulchre in Jerusalem, one can still find the largest portion of the "true cross," and splinters of it have been shared among bishops throughout the world.

This is the legacy that Saint Helena left behind. When visiting the Basilica of

Andrea Bolgi, *St. Helena*, 1630-1639, marble, St. Peter's Basilica, Rome.

St. Peter today, one will find a large marble statue of St. Helena, carved by the school of the Baroque genius, Gian Lorenzo Bernini, holding the Holy Cross.

It may have been Helena who persuaded her son to embrace Christianity as the de facto religion of the Roman Empire.

Constantine saw that his vast empire was falling apart, and believed perhaps that Christianity was the means of gluing it back together.

Religion and politics; bedfellows even in the ancient world.

Since the arrival of Saints Peter and Paul to Rome in the 1st century CE, it was among the lower classes that Christianity was most popular. The reason is simple.

Christianity proposed that the weak were strong and promised those who were worse off on earth would be better off in heaven. Moreover, early Christianity maintained that if one died for one's religion in martyrdom, instant salvation was guaranteed. These propositions captured the imaginations of the common people, a brief moment of suffering in exchange for an enternity of bliss.

Despite popular belief, there is no direct evidence that Christians were fed to the lions in the Colosseum. If that did happen, it would have been something of a halftime show. Christians would have been covered with goat's blood and sheep skins and tied to posts as ravenous lions tore them to pieces. It must have seemed out of the ordinary to the Romans to see people willingly accepting such gruesome deaths.

The Romans had never witnessed such unfathomable devotion and faith because they were pagan. They followed a polytheistic religion in which there was no sense of morality. "Religio" translates simply as "awe" or "fear."

In the ancient world, specifically for the Romans and the Greeks before them, religion meant establishing a relationship

Jean-Léon Gérôme, *The Retreating Lions*, 1902, oil on canvas, 83.2 cm x 129.5 cm, Khanenko Museum, Kyiv.

with the infinite, fostering a connection with the gods. There was no concept of a morally determining heaven or hell.

It was more of a bartering partnership. The Romans would try to strike a deal with the gods: "Okay, Jupiter, I'm going to sacrifice 12 bulls for you, and in exchange, I want a great harvest this year." It was a marketplace exchange between the divine and the human. Then along came Christianity, which proposed a pacifist philosophy. If you were struck on one cheek, simply turn the other. Such a philosophy must have seemed incomprehensible to the Romans who were a military society. By the time of Constantine, Christianity had been around for three centuries, and the more the Romans saw how devout and dedicated the Christians were, the more "en vogue" Christianity became.

Constantine may have seen Christianity as a means of pulling the Roman Empire back together. Because it is a monotheistic religion, all of Rome would fall under the guidance and protection of a single God, which would have served as a unifying force. By the early 300s CE, many of Rome's aristocrats had converted to Christianity. Paganism was falling out of favor. The word "pagan" comes from "paganos" meaning "provincial" or "rural." In other words, if you were a "paganos" it meant you were living out in the countryside, clinging to an old-fashioned polytheistic religion and worshipping Olympian gods. By that time, most of those living in the city had already converted to Christianity.

The first Christian churches built at that time, Saint Peter's, Saint Paul's Outside the Walls, Saint John Lateran and Santa Maria Maggiore, were all built outside Rome. The reason was because Christians had the unacceptable custom of burying their dead inside their churches, and for the Greeks and Romans, this practice was appalling.

The dead were always buried outside urban centers. Greeks used what was called a "necropolis" to bury their dead, with the word "necro" meaning dead and "polis" meaning city, similar in concept to a modern-day cemetery. Consider that cemeteries today are primarily enclosed detached places.

These were reintroduced by Napoleon in the early 19th century, who returned to the Greco-Roman practice of burying the dead outside the city. In the ancient world, it was the living among the living and the dead among the dead; the living and the deceased were always kept separate.

Then Christianity began to mix the two; therefore Constantine kept early Christian churches outside the city so the dead weren't mingling with the living. And at the same time, doing so was a very effective way to ease Christianity into Rome. Architecturally speaking, Christianity gradually began to take hold inside the city.

Today Saint Peter's Basilica is regarded as the global capital and seat of Catholicism. From the time of Constantine until the mid- 15th century, it was the Church of Saint John Lateran in Rome that instead served as the seat of papal power. When Constantine moved from Rome to Constantinople, the only

The Arch of Constantine.

remaining figure in the west holding anywhere near the political authority of an emperor was the pope himself. Although initially a purely spiritual figure, the pope gradually began to take on secular responsibilities, serving as an exarch for the emperor in Constantinople. The pope was tasked with various secular duties, such as arranging for grain to be imported from Egypt or maintaining the aqueducts.

Thus, the pope began to exercise secular as well as spiritual power, simply because of the power vacuum created when Constantine moved his capital east to Constantinople.

Standing under the Arch of Constantine today, it's helpful to remember that the monument was erected in 320 CE. Looking at any of the triumphal arches, it is possible to approximate the date simply based on the design. The Arch of Titus has a single opening, which signifies that it is from the earlier imperial era. The Arch of Constantine, like the Arch of Septimius Severus, has three arched openings, which means later imperial construction.

Triumphal arches also provide a clear description for whom

or by whom they were built by reading the inscription in the uppermost section, known as the "attic level."

At the top of the Arch of Constantine, the first letters that appear are I-M-P, short for "Imperator," then C-A-E-S, for "Caesar," then "Constantino Maximo" or "Emperor Caesar Constantine the Great built this."

The inscription on the Arch of Titus instead reads "Senātus Populusque Que Rōmānus" or the "Senate and the People of Rome," because the Arch of Titus was built at such an early moment in imperial Roman history that the inscription still alludes to the existence of the Roman Republic and the Senate.

Typically, triumphal arches also have imagery depicting military exploits. The Arch of Titus has images of slaves carrying

Detail from the Arch of Constantine.

the menorah out of the temple of Jerusalem. On the other side, Titus himself is participating in his own triumph.

On the Arch of Constantine, the eight roundels contain sculptural reliefs that date back to an earlier period in Roman history. At first, this dumbfounded archeologists, because most of those relief sculptures came from imperial monuments built by previous emperors such as Trajan, Hadrian, and Marcus Aurelius.

The question is, why was this artwork appropriated from one structure to another? The answer is because Constantine had taken power by force. Constantine's imperial throne was obtained by a coup. He had overthrown the previous legal incumbent. By taking artwork that had been created not only under the reign of various Roman emperors, but under the reign of the greatest Romans emperors, Trajan, Hadrian and Marcus Aurelius, Constantine was deliberately putting himself in line with the celebrated rulers that came before him.

Appropriating such artwork legitimized Constantine's illegitimate power as a usurper. This methodology in politics has continued subtly into modern times as recently as Barack Obama's inauguration. When he was sworn into office for the first time, he placed his hand on a Bible owned by Abraham Lincoln, appropriating Lincoln's reputation as a liberator and emancipator.

The second time Obama was sworn into office, he placed his hand on a stack of two Bibles, one that belonged to Lincoln and another that had belonged to Dr. Martin Luther King, Jr., associating himself with two previous highly regarded leaders and champions of equality. This is what Constantine was doing by appropriating others' historically significant art and architecture.

Consider that Constantine lived in the 300s CE and that Julius Caesar rose to power back in the middle of the 1st century BCE. When most people conceptualize Ancient Rome, they often imagine the year is 0, the presumed year of Jesus Christ's birth, but the time difference between Julius Caesar and Constantine is

360 years, more or less the amount of time that separates modern-day U.S. citizens from the pilgrims who landed at Plymouth Rock in the early 17th century or from the famous Baroque artist Caravaggio.

Almost four centuries separate Julius Caesar's rise to power from Constantine's reign. Roman civilization endured for the better part of 1,300 years.

Its peak lasted 600 years, from 200 BCE until the fall at the end of the 5th century CE. How did this fall occur? It comes down to one critical moment—Constantine's fateful decision to move the imperial seat of Rome was the harbinger that the empire would not survive. The power vacuum he created in the west eventually led to its downfall in later centuries.

That power void in the west was eventually filled when Alaric the Visigoth, leader of one of the barbarian hordes who brazenly crossed the Alps into Italian territory, sacked Rome in 410 CE. The fall of Rome is usually seen as a symbolic moment. It was anything but.

The Roman Empire was like a prize fighter in those final rounds, barely coherent but still staggering about, waiting for the final bell to ring. Rome had been sacked but would continue to languish in the west until 476 CE, when the last Roman emperor was deposed, an emperor ironically named Romulus Augustus.

Following his deposition, the barbarian Odoacer took over and made himself the king of Italy. He was an Italic king, a Christian barbarian king who ruled over what was once the western half of the Roman Empire.

However, this legendary but all-too-true story is far from over. Eventually, the east reinvaded the west when Emperor Justinian set out to regain the lost western territories in the 6th century CE.

Head, *Colossus of Constantine*, ca. 312-315 CE, marble, Palazzo dei Conservatori, Musei Capitolini, Rome.

Opposite: Interior detail of the Basilica of San Vitale in Ravenna. Photograph by Gimas.

CHAPTER 8

RAVENNA: THE BYZANTINE EMPIRE STRIKES BACK

A seismic shift occurred in the time preceding the Middle Ages with the transition from the late classical Greco-Roman world to the so- called Byzantine era. When Rome was sacked by Alaric the Visigoth in 410 CE, it was not only a physical tragedy, but also a symbolic one. The city, which had only once before been breached, fell into the hands of foreign foes, symbolically marking the end of the Roman Empire.

It was not until 476 CE, when the last Roman emperor, Romulus Augustus, was deposed that the Western Empire officially came to an end. Although the Roman empire had fallen in the west, it continued to exist in the east ever since Constantine had moved the seat of power to the new capital, Constantinople. After Rome's fall, Constantinople was the last surviving remnant of the empire for nearly a millennium until its fall in 1453 CE to Ottoman Turks and its eventual renaming as Istanbul.

What exactly led up to the fall of the western empire? In the late 4th century CE, one of Constantine's successors, Emperor

Emperor Justinian, c. 547 CE, apse mosaic, Basilica of San Vitale, Ravenna.

Theodosius I, attempted to reestablish control over the western part of the empire. Theodosius thought he could accomplish this by assigning each of his two sons the responsibility of ruling over a different geographic portion-or halves-of the empire. His son, Arcadius, was given rule over the eastern territories, the Byzantine Empire, while his other son, Honorius, was assigned to the western territories and who established his capital in Milan in Italy.

Honorius wanted to place the western capital as close as possible to the forefront of his territorial borders to defend against further barbarian incursions. The barbarians had breached the

Alps in the early 400s CE, so Honorius hoped that establishing his imperial court in Milan would ward off further potential threats.

However, Honorius soon realized that it was too late to prevent barbarians from breaching the western territories. He decided to move his entire imperial court and establish a new western capital in the city of Ravenna, located at the eastern extremity of the modern Italian region of Emilia-Romagna on the Adriatic Sea.

Why Ravenna?

First because of the city's proximity to the Adriatic. If trouble was brewing, Honorius could simply board a ship and sail across the Adriatic Sea to make his way back to the safety of Constantinople.

Second, because Ravenna possessed a very particular geological disposition. The city was surrounded by marshland, rendering it nearly impregnable. Ravenna could only be reached by those select few who knew how to navigate the difficult terrain.

Ravenna thus became capital of the western empire in 402 CE. A city that once was completely irrelevant suddenly became the seat of imperial power. Alas, Honorius was not the man for the job. He was too weak of character and historians have been acerbically critical of Honorius's attempt to salvage the western Roman empire. Eight years later, Rome was subsequently sacked, forcing Honorius to flee Ravenna and the west, abandoning Italy to the hands of barbarian kings.

Ravenna was under barbarian rule until 540 CE, the year in which one of the Byzantine emperors, Justinian, decided it was time to reconquer Italy once and for all. In 534 CE, Justinian had ordered his imperial forces to invade Italy. Their point of arrival was Sicily, which was firmly under the control of the barbarian-specifically Ostrogoth-kings. The first to rule was Odoacer in 476 CE, followed by his celebrated successor, the great

Ceiling of the Mausoleum of Galla Placidia, 425-450 CE, Basilica of San Vitale, Ravenna.

enlightened King Theodoric, who lacked Roman citizenship, but was a generally benevolent and enlightened ruler.

The city of Ravenna is an extraordinary place to experience firsthand. It embodies the transition from the late Roman classical world to the Byzantine era. Furthermore, the barbaric kings built their own monuments in the city of Ravenna, resulting in an eclectic mix of varying architectural styles.

There is architecture from the early Christian style, dating back as early as 450 CE, including the Neonian Baptistry, built under Bishop Neon, as well as a mausoleum dedicated to the daughter of Emperor Theodosius, Galla Placidia, sister of Honorius and Arcadius.

What is clear in these early 5th-century works is a monumental artistic transition. As the Roman world began to fade away, so did its values. The artistic style of the Romans reflected the ideology of classical society, but as that society began to vanish, so too did the classical arts. The idealistic reproduction of reality that characterized the classical style fell out of favor, while the Byzantine era ushered in a distinct shift toward abstraction.

The growth of Christianity also played a large role in this stylistic transition as it represented an almost escapist mentality. If the world of 5th-century Christians was anarchic and chaotic, they longed to see order and appreciated the structure and organization of the stiff mosaics that characterized this period of art. Surprisingly, the most important corpus of early Christian mosaics in the world are preserved in the city of Ravenna still today.

One can always tell the age of Justinian in his mosaic portraits by simply counting the number of his chins. The older Emperor Justinian got, the more husky he became in size and the more his chins multiplied. Ravenna also bears images of his wife, Empress Theodora. In fact, perhaps the two most famous mosaics in the world are those in the Church of San Vitale.

On one side is Emperor Justinian, and on the other, Empress Theodora, bringing their gifts to Jesus Christ. According to her contemporaries, Theodora was a stunner. The Byzantine historian Procopius claims she was allegedly a burlesque dancer earlier in her life, and then went on to become a high paid courtesan before catching the eye of Emperor Justinian and became the empress.

Indeed, to see authentic Byzantine mosaics, one does not need to visit Istanbul, because there most of the

Detail, Empress Theodora, 547 CE, mosaic, Basilica of San Vitale, Ravenna.

Byzantine mosaics have been destroyed. Instead, visit Ravenna. There, the mosaics have been almost perfectly preserved since the middle of the 6th century.

Justinian's troops were successful in conquering a strip of land extending from the northeastern corner of Italy, through Ravenna, Bologna and down through Tuscany, Umbria, Le Marche and the region known today as Lazio. Justinian's forces also recaptured Rome; connecting it all the way to Ravenna by land, and from Ravenna all the way back to Constantinople by sea. This strip of land was referred to as the "Byzantine Corridor." At that time, the representative of the Byzantine emperor in Rome was the Pope, whose position had already become secularized.

Pepin the Short, miniature, Imperial Chronicle (Anonymi chronica imperatorum), Corpus Christi College MS 373, fol. 14, ca. 1112-1114.

The pope's secularized station was widely known and was a de facto reality in Rome. The pope was now the person in charge, the figure directly representing the Byzantine emperor. The geographical reality of Italy was thus: Lombard barbarians ruling in the north; barbarians ruling in the south; and a central strip of land known as the Byzantine Corridor connected the two imperial cities of Rome and Constantinople, established by Emperor Justinian. Over the centuries, the Byzantine Corridor would gradually be transformed into the "Papal States." Moreover, in subsequent years, the pope reinforced his secular role as an earthly ruler governing the former Byzantine Corridor.

In the 8th century, another wave of barbarians, known as the Lombards, invaded the northern territory of Italy again. Pope Stephen III took it upon himself to ride north across the Alps, into an area called Gaul to ask Pépin the Short, leader of the Franks, to assist him in defending Rome from being sacked for a third time. Pépin agreed and rode his Frankish army down to defend the Eternal City.

Pépin was successful, and in exchange, was made King of the Franks. He was crowned by the pope himself, forging a long-lasting relationship between the Franks and what was then known as the Latin Christian Church. It was eventually Pépin's son, Charles Magnus ("Charles the Great") or by his French name, Charlemagne, who was coronated on Christmas day in 800 CE in the old Basilica of St. Peter and given the title of "Holy Roman Emperor."

By establishing this new royal position, the pope was attempting to resurrect the Roman Empire, but this time the new monarch would be directly subservient to Rome and to the pope-hence "Holy." Thus, there were now two major leaders in the west: Charlemagne, in the secular office of the Holy Roman Emperor, and the pope in his superior religious role. By delegating his secular duties to Charlemagne, the pope could focus on his spiritual responsibilities, leaving his earthly tasks to another leader.

This is what the pope hoped was going to happen. Instead, the office of the Holy Roman Emperor usurped nearly all secular power from the pope. Charlemagne retreated to Aachen, Germany, where he established his imperial court, and eventually a conflict arose between the pope and the Holy Roman Empire over political supremacy in the west. That conflict would continue into the later Middle Ages and eventually result in the formation of some of the most important city states in Europe, primarily in Italy-Florence, Siena, Genoa, and other medieval Italian city states that would eventually change the course of western history.

Empress Theodora and attendants, 547 CE, mosaic, Basilica of San Vitale, Ravenna.

Opposite: Giorgio Vasari, *Foundation of Florentia, a Roman Settlement*, 1563-1565, oil and wood, 540 cm x 540 cm, Palazzo Vecchio, Florence.

CHAPTER 9

THE ANCIENT ROMAN ORIGINS OF FLORENCE

Our journey through the ancient Roman world has taken us from the foundations of Rome, its transformation into a republic and then later an empire, the rise of Christianity, the fall of the empire, its continuation under the name "Byzantine Empire" and its supposed resurrection under the name "Holy Roman Empire" at the beginning of the 9th century CE.

But now, we find ourselves in medieval Florence, Italy. This may seem like a giant chronological leap, but it will soon become evident that the major players, both politically and economically, in medieval European history were not emperors or barbarian kings but instead city-states. They emerged around 1200 mainly in Italy and the most celebrated of which was Florence whose origins are interwoven with the history of ancient Rome.

The city of Florence as we know it today was founded in 59 BCE. The Romans named this new city *Florentia*, which translates as "flourishing" or "the flowering city."

To provide some historical context, 59 BCE was the same year Julius Caesar took his legions across the Alps into Gaul, launching an epic military campaign, marking the beginning of the end of the Roman republic. The reason the Romans founded Florentia was because of their increasing territories, which required cities to administer them with structures such as postal centers, bureaucratic offices and tribunals that were used to organize local government and the lives of its citizens.

Local Florentine legend maintains that so many of Julius Caesar's retiring soldiers were settling in modern-day Tuscany that the city of Florentia was born. But one thing is for certain, when the Romans built new cities, they built them as replicas of Rome, that is, the Roman archetype copied on a smaller scale. For example, in the present-day Florentine neighborhood of Santa Croce, the church celebrated for its famous tombs, there is a road called the Via Bentaccordi, which has a distinct curvilinear shape.

This was where the ancient Roman amphitheater was once located, which was, of course, much smaller than the mother of all amphitheaters, the Colosseum in Rome.

The famous Palazzo Vecchio, Florence's medieval city hall, was also built on the ruins of an ancient Roman theater, the

Ruins underneath the courtyard of Palazzo Vecchio.

Point du Gard Aqueduct.

remains of which are still visible today underneath the medieval building.

Romans were, of course, known for their fastidious hygiene. The Roman city of Florentia boasted of an unusually high number of bath complexes. To supply these baths, an 18-kilometer-long aqueduct was constructed to provide fresh water.

The spring that provided that water was just north of what today is Florence Airport. The aqueduct provided water to smaller tributaries which, in turn, distributed it throughout the city. Later in the Middle Ages, the main source of drinking water in Florence was instead the Arno River, which has always been somewhat murky and brownish in color. Yet the ancient Romans were salubrious enough to have water transported over many miles to guarantee its purity.

The central urban area of any Roman city was called the "forum." When walking through the Forum in Rome, there does not appear to be a coherent plan regarding its layout. That is because it was built over a period of almost 350 years and continual demolition and construction resulted in roads shifting around new buildings.

But when a Roman city's forum was built *ex novo,* from scratch, it had a rectangular shape, with a large open square around the perimeter of which were located all the city's major religious, social, political and economic buildings. A forum was essentially a downtown area.

The ancient Roman forum of Florence was located in the modern-day Piazza della Repubblica. Today, this piazza is most notable for its large carousel, historic cafes and the five-star hotels.

But two millennia ago, it was a large rectangular open space with one of the short sides delineated by the most important temple in Florentia dedicated to its supreme deity-Jupiter. The Temple of Jupiter Capitolinus, as it was called, was a miniature version of the Temple of Jupiter in Rome that was situated on the Capitoline Hill. The temple was located on the western side of the modern-day piazza which runs from the present-day pharmacy to the Hard Rock Café, occupying the entirety of a short side of the rectangular forum.

Of the remaining three sides, a long side ran along the front

Piazza della Repubblica.

Ponte Vecchio.

of the present-day cafes on the northern side of the piazza; the other short side of the forum ran from the present-day clock at the corner of the Cafè Gilli to the freestanding column topped with a statue; and the second longer side ran from the column back to the pharmacy. The location of a forum in a Roman city was never arbitrary. It was always situated in the exact geographical center of the city, which is still demarcated today by the freestanding column.

How did the Romans determine where the center of a city was located? Long before they laid it out, they would send surveyors to scout the land and determine the most ideal location to build their city.

The reason behind Florence's placement in the Arno River valley lies with the location of the celebrated medieval bridge, the Ponte Vecchio, which was built in the 1330s.

The medieval Ponte Vecchio actually replaced an earlier ancient Roman bridge. Ancient Romans first realized that this was the narrowest point of the river in this area, and the most convenient place to build a bridge. Therefore, there has been a bridge spanning that particular spot of the Arno River for the last two millennia.

The surveyors essentially determined that this was where the main ancient north-south road needed to be situated, in line with that bridge. In ancient Roman cities, the major north-south road was known as the *cardo*. The reason was that if you were either north or south of Rome, this road would lead you back to the capital- the beating heart of all the territory, of power and empire. That *cardo* is still very much present in modern-day Florence and is appropriately named the Via Roma.

Most have heard the cliché that all roads lead to Rome. There is quite a bit of truth to that hyperbole. Approximately 400,000 kilometers (250,000 miles) of roadways were laid by the Romans, of which nearly 80,500 kilometers (50,000 miles) were paved. An extraordinary undertaking by any standards. While the north-south road was known as the *cardo,* the east-west road was known as the *decumanus*. Both ancient roads are still very much present in Florence.

The decumanus once ran westward through the 19th-century neoclassical archway on the western side of the Piazza della Repubblica and eastward along the present-day Via del Corso, which eventually turns into Borgo degli Albizi. The decumanus would intersect with the cardo, and that point of intersection marked the exact geographical center of a Roman city, which is where the ancient forum of Florence was going to be laid out.

Essentially, the column in the Piazza della Repubblica, which marks the point of intersection of those two roads, has been marking the center of Florence for the last 2,000 years. The statue standing on top of the column represents "Dovizia" who holds a cornucopia in her hands symbolizing "Abundance."

In the current age of Google Maps, which provide routes so direct we might as well be wearing horse-blinders, we seldom look at a real map anymore. However, the importance of studying a paper map of any new city is to truly orient oneself as to where you are. The urban layout of a city reveals quite a bit about its history and urbanism.

In ancient Florentia, the streets followed a grid pattern, or an orthogonal city plan, the origins of which might be surprising. In the same way that today the United States has trickle-down military or space technology, everyday life in the ancient world also benefitted from military developments. Florentia was laid out the same way that a rectangular Roman military camp, or *castrum*, was. Uniform tents were set up to create units, separated by streets or avenues which facilitated the movement of troops. Grid-patterned cities were based on the same grids as those in military camps, *castra* in the plural. In the Roman cities of Florentia (Florence), Luca (Lucca) and Pisarum (Pisa), the castrum layout is present. Since the Romans also exported this type of urban development, English cities with names ending in a castra-sound, like Leicester, Gloucester, or Worcester, were indeed also once Roman cities with the castrum layout. Moreover, this philosophy of urbanism is one that is still very much alive today in places like New York City.

Looking at a map of Florence today, you can still see the borders of the Roman city, which was considerably smaller than the city is today. The street running along the north side of Florence

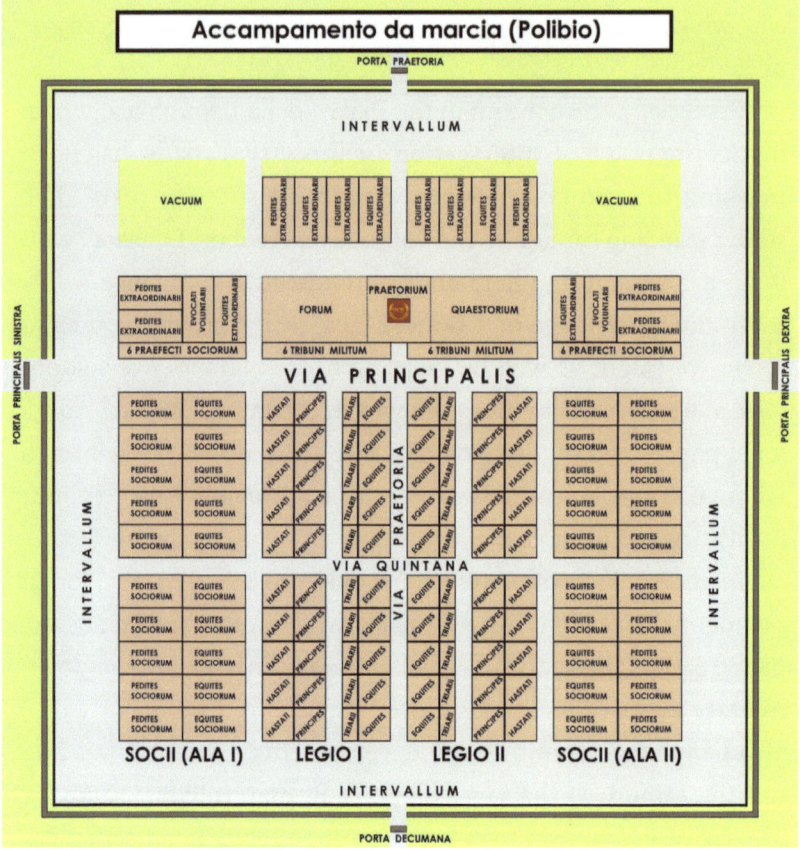

Cristiano64, CC BY-SA 3.0, via Wikimedia Commons.

Cathedral was the northern border of the city; while the western extremity was the modern-day Via Tornabuoni; the eastern border ran along the current-day Via del Proconsolo and in front of the museum known as the Bargello. Archeologists argue whether there was a southern wall, since the river could serve as a natural boundary.

Some believe that if it did exist, it ran along the present-day Via Porta Rossa, because this street extends all the way to the western Via Tornabuoni and the eastern Via del Proconsolo. Others argue instead that there was no need for a southern wall because the river served as a natural defensive border.

We now have an idea of the approximate scale of the ancient Roman city of Florentia, which had a population of around 10,000 people. But why name it "the flowering city?" Some believe it was because of the booming demographics of ancient Florence. It was a city that was built from the ground up with a soaring population in less than a century.

While the more romantic myth was that the name Florentia came from the very beautiful lilies, the *gigli*, which grew along the Arno River valley. It is still the symbol of Florence today. Eventually, Florentia became Fiorenza in the Middle Ages, Firenze in the 19th century, and finally into the anglicized "Florence" of today. All four names mean the same thing, "the flowering city." Ultimately, Florentia's destiny was inextricably linked to the fate of Rome itself.

When the empire finally fell in the 5th century CE because of continuous barbarian incursions, people living in Roman cities abandoned them to seek safety in isolation. They moved to the countryside where it was more difficult to be discovered by violent groups like the Huns, the Vandals, the Ostrogoths, the Visigoths and the Lombards. With Roman cities abandoned, they gradually fell into disrepair. Vegetation took over and buildings began to slowly crumble. Urbanism was thus expunged from not just Florentia, but just about all European cities for approximately 500 years. In fact, it was not until around 1000 CE that people began to slowly migrate back into the cities and to rebuild them.

One of the most crucial parts of any thriving ancient or medieval metropolis was a functional marketplace. The people who first resettled Florence in the 11th century took advantage of the large, abandoned rectangular plot of land that was once the forum to build a central market. Today, markets are considered romantic and charming, however, a medieval market would be congested and unsanitary, the smell nauseating and hygiene non-existent. Building a market on what was once an ancient Roman forum is the modern equivalent of building a Walmart on top of Capitol Hill in Washington, DC.

Depictions from the 18th and 19th centuries show the still extant marketplace in the Piazza della Repubblica with the column erupting above the stalls and stands. That market continued to function in the present-day Piazza della Repubblica until 1861, which was the year of unification, the Risorgimento, when the Italy became a nation.

The fall of the Roman Empire had been the last time that

Filippo Napoletano, *View of Florence with the Old Market Square*, ca. 1600-1630, oil on canvas, 115 cm x 193 cm, Banca CR Firenze, Florence.

the entire geographic peninsula was under the control of a single ruler. In the Middle Ages, between nine to twelve different sovereign states emerged, and during this time, Florence was a city-state. It was a city but also an independent sovereign country. Other Italian city-states included Siena and Venice, while the pope controlled most of central Italy. There was a duke in Milan and Urbino, and a king in Naples. They were essentially neighboring sovereign entities sharing one boot-shaped geographical peninsula.

All that changed in 1861 when a single king took control over the entire country, King Victor Emmanuel II, who attained power with the aid of the charismatic general Giuseppe Garibaldi. When this happened, one of the most pressing matters was to establish a national capital. The logical city to serve as such was Rome. But the pope at the time wanted nothing to do with "Italy." Should he join the Italian nation, the pope would lose all his territories and, therefore, all his secular power. Consequently, all diplomatic relations were cut off between the Vatican and the new nation of Italy-a political situation comparable to an in-house divorce.

It would have been embarrassing for the new king to set up his nation's capital next to the head of the religion to which 99% of his subjects adhered. So, they looked for another solution. Florence was chosen as the nation's interim capital in 1865 and served as such for the next five years-a period known as the "Firenze Capitale" era. The advantage of Florence was that it was positioned just about halfway down the Italian peninsula.

Geographically speaking, it was the most conveniently located city. The disadvantage was that it was a city characterized by medieval architecture, which had to be rectified with modern upgrades. They returned to the place where the history of Florence began-the ancient Roman forum known today as Piazza della Repubblica.

The plan was to demolish the then-functioning market and

all the surrounding medieval buildings. They rebuilt the area in a neoclassical style of architecture, which is, indeed, what stands today. Many people are misguidedly in awe of the neoclassical architecture when they visit Florence today. They commend the buildings for their resilience through time, but the buildings date to the late 19th century and are only about a century and a half old! To the untrained eye, this is an easy oversight. However, one of the goals of this book is to provide the reader with the tools necessary to overcome these types of conclusions.

If you look around the piazza, you will find a date that explicitly indicates the 19th-century chronology of the architecture etched in Roman numerals directly above the arch that leads out of the piazza:

MDCCCXCV.

- "M" is the Roman numeral for 1,000
- "D" is 500, like a demi-millennium, followed by
- "CCC" each of which is 100 (1,000+ 500+300= 1800)
- "X" is the Roman numeral for 10
- "C" is 100 (Subtract the smaller numeral from the larger=90)
- "V" is 5

The total sum of which is 1895.

While in the United States, we believe that the only practical application for Roman numerals is a Superbowl, you will discover an even greater usage if you ever take a *girata* (a spin) around Europe and find yourself able to read the dates of famous architectural monuments.

The uppermost section of a triumphal arch is called the attic level. In ancient Rome, if you read the inscription on the attic of

a triumphal arch, you can figure out for whom or by whom it was built. This holds true in the 19th century neoclassical triumphal arch in Florence as well. The three lines of the attic inscription reveal the entire history of the piazza.

It reads: *"L'antico centro della citta"* or "the ancient center of the city" referring to the Roman forum which once occupied the space. The second line reads *"Da secolare squallore."* "Da" means "from," and "Secolare" sounds similar to the English word "secular." When something is secular, it is not divine, but temporal. "Secular" in English comes from the Latin "secularum," which is a unit of time that means "century."

Centuries of squallore, or "squalor." This refers to the marketplace that once functioned there. The final line is climactic: "A vita nuova restituito" – "To new life restored." This dramatic ending refers to the revamping in the modernized neoclassical style, which, in turn, echoes the greatness of the piazza's ancient Roman origins.

Henry Holday, *Dante and Beatrice*, 1883, oil on canvas, 142.2 cm x 203.2 cm, Walker Art Gallery, Liverpool.

The entire inscription's translation is: "The ancient center of the city, from centuries of squalor to new life restored." In just three concise verses it recounts the entire two-millennium history of this urban space.

Despite the practical brevity of this three-sentence history lesson, few people even bother to read the inscription, and particularly its last line which includes the words *"a vita nuova."*

Nuova, is the Italian adjective which means "new" in English and can be used either before or after a noun, depending on the desired emphasis. In this case, it's *vita nuova* because there is a historical literary allusion to a work of poetry published in 1295 by Florence's most celebrated medieval poet, Dante Alighieri. Dante's greatest work, *The Divine Comedy*, was a trilogy published in

Domenico di Michelino, *Dante Alighieri with Florence and the Realms of the Divine Comedy (Hell, Purgatory, Paradise)*, 1465, oil on canvas, 232 cm x 290 cm, Florence Cathedral, Florence.

1314. But his first publication was a work of poetry called *La Vita Nuova*, dedicated to his beloved Beatrice and published in 1295.

Why allude to Dante in this inscription?

Because most believe that Dante was the artistic catalyst that marks the beginning of the period known as the Renaissance. This poet essentially produced one of the most extraordinary literary works in history, seemingly out of the blue. What Dante started with the beginning of the Renaissance was completed 600 years later in 1895 with the revamping of the piazza and its restoration to its original ancient glory.

I daresay that only around one in one thousand people pick up on the Dante allusion in the inscription. And that is why the

Piazza della Repubblica is an ideal introduction to the whole city of Florence and its great history.

This urban space set the tone for one of the most sophisticated and beautiful cities in the world, and the further one delves into history, beginning with Ancient Rome, through the Middle Ages and the Renaissance, and eventually to our own day, the more one will be able to appreciate this extraordinary beauty.

ABOUT THE AUTHOR...

Dr. Rocky Ruggiero has been a professor of art and architectural history since 1999, sharing his knowledge and passion for Italian art with eager students, both in universities and on private excursions. His ongoing connections often allow his participants unique after- hours entry to places many tourists are not allowed, such as the Sistine Chapel, as well as front-row balcony seats at Siena's annual Palio horse race, and most recently and hour-long private tour of Leonardo's "Last Supper" in Milan.

He received his BA from the College of the Holy Cross and a Master of Arts degree from Syracuse University, where he was awarded a prestigious Florence Fellowship in 1996. He furthered his art historical studies at the University of Exeter, UK, where he received a PhD in Art History and Visual Culture. He is also the author of the book *Brunelleschi's Basilica: The Building of Santo Spirito in Florence*.

Dr. Ruggiero lived in Florence, Italy, for 20 years where he lectured for American universities including Syracuse, Kent State, Vanderbilt, and Boston College. Dr. Ruggiero has written and starred in several television documentaries on his expertise in the Italian Renaissance. He has appeared as an expert witness for NBC News, as well as in the History Channel's "Engineering an Empire: Da Vinci's World," "Museum Secrets: the Uffizi Gallery," and the NatGeo/NOVA PBS program "Great Cathedral Mystery." His last two documentaries, "Florence: The Art of Magnificence," and "Medici: The Art of Power" aired nationally on PBS.

As an academic advisory board member of the non-profit group Friends of Florence and frequent lecturer for Friends of the Uffizi Gallery, he has been instrumental in encouraging fundraising for the restoration of works of art throughout the city.

Dr. Ruggiero now lives in the U.S. where he offers online art history courses and educational webinars, as well as in-person lectures and cultural events throughout the U.S. and Italy on the Renaissance.

In Italy, Dr. Ruggiero leads private excursions and week-long travel programs throughout Italy, offering participants a first-class experience in a close-up encounter with art, architecture and culture, in addition to fine accommodations with like-minded art aficionados.

For information on his travel tours, online courses, video lectures, documentaries, blogs and podcasts visit rockyruggiero.com.

www.ingramcontent.com/pod-product-compliance
Lightning Source LLC
Chambersburg PA
CBHW041805160426
43191CB00004B/58